Fun Food

RDA ENTHUSIAST BRANDS, LLC
MILWAUKEE, WI

Fun Food

EDITORIAL
EDITOR-IN-CHIEF Catherine Cassidy
CREATIVE DIRECTOR Howard Greenberg
EDITORIAL OPERATIONS DIRECTOR Kerri Balliet

MANAGING EDITOR/PRINT & DIGITAL BOOKS Mark Hagen
ASSOCIATE CREATIVE DIRECTOR Edwin Robles Jr.

ASSOCIATE EDITOR Molly Jasinski
ART DIRECTOR Catherine Fletcher
EDITORIAL PRODUCTION MANAGER Dena Ahlers
COPY CHIEF Deb Warlaumont Mulvey
COPY EDITOR Dulcie Shoener
CONTRIBUTING COPY EDITOR Steph Kilen

FOOD EDITORS James Schend; Peggy Woodward, RD
RECIPE EDITORS Mary King; Jenni Sharp, RD; Irene Yeh
CONTENT OPERATIONS MANAGER Colleen King
CONTENT OPERATIONS ASSISTANT Shannon Stroud
EDITORIAL SERVICES ADMINISTRATOR Marie Brannon

TEST KITCHEN & FOOD STYLING MANAGER
Sarah Thompson
TEST COOKS Nicholas Iverson (lead), Matthew Hass,
Lauren Knoelke
FOOD STYLISTS Kathryn Conrad (senior), Shannon Roum,
Leah Rekau
PREP COOKS Megumi Garcia, Melissa Hansen,
Bethany Van Jacobson, Sara Wirtz

PHOTOGRAPHY DIRECTOR Stephanie Marchese
PHOTOGRAPHERS Dan Roberts, Jim Wieland
PHOTOGRAPHER/SET STYLIST Grace Natoli Sheldon
SET STYLISTS Stacey Genaw, Melissa Haberman, Dee Dee Jacq
PHOTO STUDIO ASSISTANT Ester Robards

EDITORIAL BUSINESS MANAGER Kristy Martin
EDITORIAL BUSINESS ASSOCIATE Samantha Lea Stoeger

EDITOR, *TASTE OF HOME* Jeanne Ambrose
ASSOCIATE CREATIVE DIRECTOR, *TASTE OF HOME* Erin Burns
ART DIRECTOR, *TASTE OF HOME* Kristin Bowker

BUSINESS
GENERAL MANAGER, TASTE OF HOME COOKING SCHOOL
Erin Puariea
EXECUTIVE PRODUCER, TASTE OF HOME ONLINE
COOKING SCHOOL Karen Berner

THE READER'S DIGEST ASSOCIATION, INC.
PRESIDENT AND CHIEF EXECUTIVE OFFICER Bonnie Kintzer
CHIEF FINANCIAL OFFICER Colette Chestnut
VICE PRESIDENT, CHIEF OPERATING OFFICER, NORTH AMERICA
Howard Halligan
VICE PRESIDENT, ENTHUSIAST BRANDS, BOOKS & RETAIL
Harold Clarke
CHIEF MARKETING OFFICER Leslie Dukker Doty
SENIOR VICE PRESIDENT, GLOBAL HR & COMMUNICATIONS
Phyllis E. Gebhardt, SPHR
VICE PRESIDENT, BRAND MARKETING Beth Gorry
VICE PRESIDENT, CHIEF TECHNOLOGY OFFICER
Aneel Tejwaney
VICE PRESIDENT, CONSUMER MARKETING PLANNING
Jim Woods

COVER PHOTOGRAPHY
PHOTOGRAPHER Dan Roberts
FOOD STYLIST Sarah Thompson
SET STYLIST Melissa Haberman

© 2015 RDA ENTHUSIAST BRANDS, LLC
1610 N. 2ND ST., SUITE 102, MILWAUKEE WI 53212-3906

INTERNATIONAL STANDARD BOOK NUMBER: 978-1-61765-458-9

LIBRARY OF CONGRESS CONTROL NUMBER: 2015933130

COMPONENT NUMBER: 116000215H.00.75

ALL RIGHTS RESERVED.

TASTE OF HOME IS A REGISTERED TRADEMARK OF THE
READER'S DIGEST ASSOCIATION, INC.

PRINTED IN CHINA
1 3 5 7 9 10 8 6 4 2

PICTURED ON THE FRONT COVER (CLOCKWISE FROM
TOP LEFT): Best Friend Cupcakes (p. 96), Petal Cupcakes (p. 92),
Give a Hoot Cupcakes (p. 88), Flutter By Cupcakes (p. 95),
Wedding Shower Cupcakes (p. 104), Call Me Leo Cupcakes (p. 100)

PICTURED ON THE BACK COVER (FROM TOP):
Bunny Pancakes (p. 72), Watermelon Shark (p. 62),
Chicken Alphabet Soup (p. 62)

20

12

16

8

91

Let the Fun Begin!

Who said you can't play with your food? Invite the kids into the kitchen, because this cookbook is perfect for little hands and big appetites. *Taste of Home Fun Food* transforms mealtime prep into an activity the whole family will love...with delicious results!

There's so much to try inside, you won't know where to start! Six colorful chapters offer the perfect recipes for everyday meals, special occasions, classroom treats and more. Better yet, all 170+ recipes come from home cooks like you.

You'll have plenty of options for every course. Breakfast will never be the same once you make **Peanut Butter & Banana Waffles** (p. 25) or **Jolly Jelly Doughnuts** (p. 23). Dig in to **Fruit Salsa with Cinnamon Chips** (p. 17) or **Veggie Cheese People** (p. 11) for party-time appetizers or after-school snacks. Try something new and get creative with your main dishes, such as **Family Quilt Pizza** (p. 43), **Hot Dog Speed Racer** (p. 34) and **Popcorn & Pretzel Chicken Tenders** (p. 46).

Don't forget about dessert! Wow the crowd when you bring out **Birthday Clown Cake** (p. 103) or **Cool Watermelon Pops** (p. 100) at your big event. The bake sale crowd will go crazy for **Ultimate Candy Bar Cookies** (p. 105) and **Lady Bug Chocolate Cupcakes** (p. 90). You'll be serving up seconds before you know it!

You'll also notice lots of special bonus recipes sprinkled throughout the book. Check out the oh-so-adorable **Bunny Pancakes** (p. 72) or **July 4th Layered Drinks** (p. 74). These little treats will add an extra dose of fun to your next gathering.

Enjoy creating new favorites! *Taste of Home Fun Food* is sure to become a well-loved cookbook in your home, so gather the family for some homemade memories!

66

70

77

16

68

Contents

DISCOVER MORE KID-FRIENDLY RECIPES
ON FACEBOOK, PINTEREST & TWITTER

f LIKE US
facebook.com/tasteofhome

TWEET US
@tasteofhome

SHOP WITH US
shoptasteofhome.com

 FOLLOW US
pinterest.com/taste_of_home

SHARE A RECIPE
tasteofhome.com/submit

Kid-Approved Sippers & Snacks

Keep little (and big) appetites satisfied! Whether you need a snack after school, before a game or just for fun, these silly bites and beverages do the trick.

Apple and Peanut Butter Stackers

1. In a large bowl, combine the first six ingredients. In a microwave or heavy saucepan over low heat, melt baking chips with oil; stir until smooth.

2. Pour over popcorn mixture and toss to coat. Immediately spread onto two baking sheets; let stand until set, about 2 hours. Store in airtight containers.

Watermelon Sherbet Smoothies

These fast-to-fix smoothies have become a summertime tradition for my sons. There's nothing quite as cool as these chilly drinks when it comes to beating the heat.
—JAMIE COCKEREL KALAMAZOO, MI

START TO FINISH: 10 MIN.
MAKES: 4 SERVINGS

- 3 cups cubed seedless watermelon
- 1 cup crushed ice
- 1 cup watermelon, raspberry or lime sherbet
- 4 teaspoons lime juice
- 2 teaspoons miniature semisweet chocolate chips

In a blender, combine the watermelon, ice, sherbet and lime juice; cover and process for 30 seconds or until smooth. Stir if necessary. Pour into chilled glasses; sprinkle with chocolate chips. Serve immediately.

Pirate Punch

Come sail away! A frothy tropical fruit and lime sherbet punch takes you straight to party paradise.
—*TASTE OF HOME* TEST KITCHEN

START TO FINISH: 10 MIN.
MAKES: 21 SERVINGS (¾ CUP EACH)

- 1 can (46 ounces) unsweetened pineapple juice
- ¾ cup frozen limeade concentrate, thawed
- 1 bottle (1 liter) ginger ale, chilled
- 1 quart lime sherbet, softened

In a punch bowl, combine pineapple juice and limeade concentrate. Add soda and sherbet; stir until blended. Serve immediately.

Apple and Peanut Butter Stackers

The best way to get kids interested in cooking and eating right is to let them lend a helping hand. Sliced apple "sandwiches" are one way to pique their interest and kitchen creativity, all while giving them something good to snack on.
—SHIRLEY WARREN THIENSVILLE, WI

START TO FINISH: 10 MIN.
MAKES: 6 SERVINGS

- 2 medium apples
- ⅓ cup chunky peanut butter
  Optional fillings: granola, miniature semisweet chocolate chips and M&M's minis

Core apples. Cut each apple crosswise into six slices. Spread peanut butter over six slices; sprinkle with fillings of your choice. Top with remaining apple slices.

White Chocolate Party Mix

I get rave reviews every time I prepare this crispy combo of cereal, popcorn, pretzels, nuts and candies. Coated in white chocolate, it's perfect for meetings, parties and gift giving.
—ROSE WENTZEL ST. LOUIS, MO

PREP: 10 MIN. + STANDING • **COOK:** 5 MIN.
MAKES: 9½ QUARTS

- 16 cups popped popcorn
- 3 cups Frosted Cheerios
- 1 package (10 ounces) fat-free pretzel sticks
- 2 cups milk chocolate M&M's (about 12 ounces)
- 1½ cups pecan halves
- 1 package (8 ounces) milk chocolate English toffee bits or brickle toffee bits
- 2 packages (10 to 12 ounces each) white baking chips
- 2 tablespoons canola oil

Palm Tree Straws

To make palm tree straws, first go to **tasteofhome.com/halloweenprint** for the printable pattern. Trace leaf pattern with 1-in. stem onto card stock. Cut out leaves. Use clear tape to stick 5 or 6 leaves around a straw a few inches from the top.

Pirate Punch

Ogre Eyes Hot Cocoa

Here's looking at you! Guests of all ages will get a kick out of this eerie drink staring back at them.

—JEANNIE KLUGH LANCASTER, PA

START TO FINISH: 25 MIN.
MAKES: 8 SERVINGS

 8 **cups milk**
 1 **cup mint chocolate chips**
 1 **cup instant hot cocoa mix**
 16 **large marshmallows**
 16 **Crows candies**
 16 **lollipop sticks**

1. In a large saucepan, combine 1 cup milk, chocolate chips and cocoa mix. Cook and stir over low heat until chips are melted. Stir in remaining milk; heat through.

2. Meanwhile, cut a slit in top of each marshmallow; insert a candy. Carefully insert a lollipop stick through the bottom of each marshmallow and into each candy.

3. Pour hot cocoa into mugs or cups; place two prepared marshmallows in each cup. Serve immediately.

NOTE *If mint chocolate chips are not available, place 2 cups (12 ounces) semisweet chocolate chips and ¼ teaspoon peppermint extract in a plastic bag; seal and toss to coat. Allow chips to stand for 24-48 hours.*

TOP TIP

The trick to keep marshmallows from going stale? I freeze them. When I know I'll need them for a recipe, I take them out of the freezer and let them thaw out for a while. They'll taste just as fresh.

—**LYN C.** PROVO, UT

**Ogre Eyes
Hot Cocoa**

Fruity Frappe

My frappe gets all of its sweetness from berries, orange juice and honey. It's a beverage to get you moving!
—**PATRICIA CROUSE** WARREN, PA

START TO FINISH: 10 MIN.
MAKES: 4 SERVINGS

- 1 **cup water**
- 1 **cup fat-free milk**
- ⅔ **cup thawed orange juice concentrate**
- 3 **tablespoons honey**
- ½ **teaspoon vanilla extract**
- 1 **cup ice cubes**
- 1 **cup frozen unsweetened mixed berries**

Place all ingredients in a blender; cover and process until blended. Serve immediately.

Waffled Pizza Bites

The whole family will love this playful twist on waffles. Mozzarella and Parmesan cheeses are sandwiched between two layers of dough and cooked up in the waffle iron. It's like a pizza-grilled-cheese-waffle sandwich!
—**DEIRDRE COX** KANSAS CITY, MO

START TO FINISH: 20 MIN.
MAKES: 8 APPETIZERS (1¾ CUPS SAUCE)

- 1¼ **cups shredded part-skim mozzarella cheese**
- ¼ **cup shredded Parmesan cheese**
- ½ **teaspoon dried basil**
- ½ **teaspoon dried oregano**
- 2 **tubes (8 ounces each) refrigerated crescent rolls**
- 32 **slices pepperoni (about 2 ounces)**
- 1 **jar (14 ounces) pizza sauce, warmed**
  Optional toppings: sliced pepperoni, shredded mozzarella cheese and basil

1. In a small bowl, combine the cheeses, basil and oregano. Separate each roll of crescent dough into two 7x6-in. rectangles; seal perforations.
2. Place one rectangle on a preheated greased 8-in.-square waffle iron (dough will not cover entire surface). Layer with half the cheese mixture and half the pepperoni to ½ in. of edges; top with another rectangle.

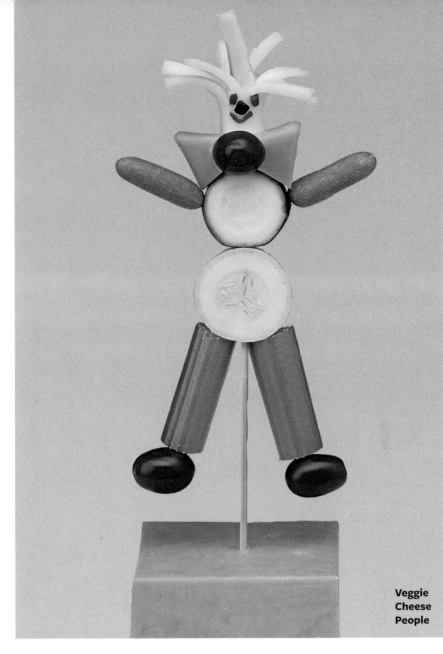

Veggie Cheese People

Bake for 4-5 minutes or until golden brown. Repeat.
3. Remove to a cutting board and cool slightly. Cut into triangles; serve warm with pizza sauce and, if desired, toppings.

Veggie Cheese People

Let your imagination run wild with this recipe. Mix and match cheese and vegetables to your heart's content.
—**TASTE OF HOME** TEST KITCHEN

START TO FINISH: 30 MIN.
MAKES: 12 SERVINGS

- 1 **cup baby carrots**
- 3 **celery ribs**
- 1 **cup cherry tomatoes or grape tomatoes**
- 1 **small zucchini and yellow summer squash**
- 1 **medium sweet yellow, red or green pepper**
- 5 **miniature dill or sweet pickles**
- ¼ **cup sliced pimiento-stuffed olives**
- ¼ **cup pitted ripe olives**
- 2 **hard-cooked eggs**
  Pimientos
- 3 **string cheese**
  Block cheddar cheese
  Wooden skewers and toothpicks

Cut vegetables and cheese into desired shapes. To create people, thread the shapes onto skewers; use toothpicks to attach arms and legs. Insert skewers into a block of cheese.

Caramel
Apple Cider Float

1. In a small bowl, combine the flour, cornmeal, baking powder, salt and onion powder; cut in shortening until crumbly. Whisk milk and egg; stir into flour mixture just until moistened. Dip sausages into batter.

2. In an electric skillet or deep fryer, heat oil to 375°. Fry sausages, a few at a time, for 2-3 minutes or until golden brown. Drain on paper towels. Serve with ketchup.

Chocolate-Hazelnut Fruit Pizza

You can prepare this snackable pizza in just 10 minutes! What better way to sneak in some daily servings of fruit?

—DALYNN DOWLING GRAND FORKS AFB, ND

START TO FINISH: 10 MIN.
MAKES: 4 SERVINGS

1	whole wheat tortilla (8 inches)
2	tablespoons Nutella
3	to 4 fresh strawberries, sliced
½	medium firm banana, peeled and sliced
½	medium kiwifruit, peeled and sliced

Spread tortilla with Nutella. Arrange the fruits over the top. Cut into four wedges. Serve immediately.

Chocolate-Hazelnut Fruit Pizza

Caramel Apple Cider Float

Who doesn't love the flavors of caramel, apples and vanilla ice cream together? If I'm feeling fancy, I drizzle caramel syrup around the inside of my glass before adding the apple cider and ginger ale.

—CINDY REAMS PHILIPSBURG, PA

START TO FINISH: 10 MIN.
MAKES: 2 SERVINGS

1	cup chilled apple cider or unsweetened apple juice
1	cup chilled ginger ale or lemon-lime soda
1	cup vanilla ice cream
2	tablespoons caramel sundae syrup

Divide cider and ginger ale between two glasses. Top with ice cream; drizzle with caramel syrup.

Miniature Corn Dogs

These little corn dogs add deliciousness to any occasion. You can definitely expect them to disappear fast when you set them out for a gathering.

—DEB PERRY BLUFFTON, IN

PREP: 25 MIN. • **COOK:** 5 MIN./BATCH
MAKES: ABOUT 3½ DOZEN

1	cup all-purpose flour
2	tablespoons cornmeal
1½	teaspoons baking powder
¼	teaspoon salt
	Dash onion powder
3	tablespoons shortening
¾	cup 2% milk
1	egg
1	package (16 ounces) miniature smoked sausages
	Oil for deep-fat frying
	Spicy ketchup

Costume Crackers

Mini-Burger Potato Bites

The caramelized onions and creamy sauce make these yummy bites a huge hit. Folks have told me that these appetizers are better than any similar sliders they've had at restaurants.

—**MARIBETH CONDO** LINDENHURST, IL

PREP: 40 MIN. • **BROIL:** 5 MIN.
MAKES: 16 APPETIZERS

- 16 **frozen waffle-cut fries**
- 2 **medium onions, cut into ⅛-inch slices**
- 1 **tablespoon butter**
- 1 **tablespoon olive oil**
- 1 **teaspoon sugar**
- ½ **teaspoon salt**
- ⅛ **teaspoon pepper**
- 1 **pound ground beef**
- 2 **teaspoons steak seasoning**
- 3 **egg yolks**
- 4½ **teaspoons lemon juice**
- 1½ **teaspoons water**
- ½ **cup butter, melted**
- 4 **slices cheddar cheese, quartered**
  Optional toppings: tomatoes and pickles

1. Bake waffle fries according to package directions. In a large skillet, cook onions in butter and oil over medium heat for 10 minutes. Add the sugar, salt and pepper; cook 3-5 minutes longer or until onions are golden brown, stirring frequently.
2. Meanwhile, in a large bowl, combine beef and steak seasoning. Shape into 16 patties. Cook in a large skillet until a thermometer reads 160° and juices run clear, turning once.
3. For sauce, in a double boiler or metal bowl over simmering water, constantly whisk the egg yolks, lemon juice and water until mixture reaches 160° or is thick enough to coat the back of a metal spoon. Reduce heat to low. Slowly drizzle in warm melted butter, whisking constantly.
4. Top each waffle fry with a burger and cheese. Broil 4-5 in. from the heat for 1-2 minutes or until cheese is melted. Top with onions, sauce and, if desired, additional toppings.
NOTE *This recipe was tested with McCormick's Montreal Steak Seasoning. Look for it in the spice aisle.*

Costume Crackers

Try out any alter ego your heart desires... then eat your disguise! The different shape possibilities are endless.

—*TASTE OF HOME* **TEST KITCHEN**

START TO FINISH: 30 MIN.
MAKES: 6 SERVINGS

- 6 **flour and/or sun-dried tomato tortillas (10 inches)**
- 3 **tablespoons butter, melted**
- ½ **teaspoon dried basil**
- ½ **teaspoon dried thyme**
- ¼ **teaspoon seasoned salt**
- ¼ **teaspoon garlic powder**
- ⅛ **teaspoon pepper**

1. Brush both sides of tortillas with butter. Combine the remaining ingredients; sprinkle over one side of tortillas. Cut shapes such as mustaches, bow ties or horns from tortillas; discard scraps.
2. Place on ungreased baking sheets. Bake at 400° for 7-9 minutes or until crisp.

Mozzarella Sticks

Who knew something this easy could taste so fantastic? Crunchy on the outside with gooey melted cheese on the inside, this favorite appetizer will be a big hit. The kids can help wrap the string cheese, too.

—**SHIRLEY WARREN** THIENSVILLE, WI

START TO FINISH: 20 MIN.
MAKES: 1 DOZEN

- 12 **pieces string cheese**
- 12 **egg roll wrappers**
  Oil for deep-fat frying
  Marinara or spaghetti sauce

1. Place a piece of string cheese near the bottom corner of one egg roll wrapper (keep remaining wrappers covered with a damp paper towel until ready to use). Fold bottom corner over cheese. Roll up halfway; fold sides toward center over cheese. Moisten remaining corner with water; roll up tightly to seal. Repeat with remaining wrappers and cheese.
2. In an electric skillet, heat ½ in. of oil to 375°. Fry sticks, a few at a time, for 30-60 seconds on each side or until golden brown. Drain on paper towels. Serve with marinara sauce.

Monster Curried Cheese Ball

Don't be scared of this cheese ball! You can't beat the combination of bold chutney with mellow cheddar and blue cheeses. Be sure to make it the day before serving so it can sit in the refrigerator overnight.
—*TASTE OF HOME* TEST KITCHEN

PREP: 20 MIN. + CHILLING
MAKES: 2½ CUPS

- ½ cup mango chutney
- ½ teaspoon curry powder
- 1 package (8 ounces) cream cheese, softened
- 8 ounces sharp white cheddar cheese, shredded
- 1 package (4 ounces) crumbled blue cheese, softened
  Coarsely shredded red cabbage, green pepper pieces, baby carrot and radish
  Assorted crackers

1. In a blender, cover and process the chutney and curry until pureed. In a small bowl, combine the cheeses and chutney mixture; beat until blended. Shape into a ball; wrap tightly in plastic wrap. Refrigerate overnight.
2. Place on a plate. Add the monster's hair and face, using the cabbage, green pepper, carrot and radish. Serve with crackers.

Mini Hot Dogs 'n' Meatballs

Since this recipe's so popular, I usually double it right away. Try increasing the heat factor by using a spicier barbecue or spaghetti sauce. Make it your own!
—ANDREA CHAMBERLAIN MACEDON, NY

PREP: 5 MIN. • **COOK:** 3 HOURS
MAKES: 8 CUPS

- 1 package (12 ounces) frozen fully cooked Italian meatballs
- 1 package (16 ounces) miniature hot dogs or smoked sausages
- 1 package (3½ ounces) sliced pepperoni
- 1 jar (24 ounces) meatless spaghetti sauce
- 1 bottle (18 ounces) barbecue sauce
- 1 bottle (12 ounces) chili sauce

In a 5-qt. slow cooker, combine all ingredients. Cover and cook on low for 3-4 hours or until heated through.

Pizza Roll-Ups

This has been a regular after-school snack in my house since I first got the recipe through 4-H Club. The bite-size pizza treats are especially good served with spaghetti sauce for dipping.
—DONNA KLETTKE WHEATLAND, MO

PREP: 20 MIN. • **BAKE:** 15 MIN.
MAKES: 2 DOZEN

- ½ pound ground beef
- 1 can (8 ounces) tomato sauce
- ½ cup shredded part-skim mozzarella cheese
- ½ teaspoon dried oregano
- 2 tubes (8 ounces each) refrigerated crescent rolls

1. In a large skillet, cook beef over medium heat until no longer pink; drain. Remove from heat. Add tomato sauce, mozzarella cheese and oregano.
2. Separate crescent dough into eight rectangles, pinching seams together. Place about 3 tablespoons of meat mixture along one long side of each rectangle. Roll up, jelly-roll style, starting with a long side. Cut each roll into three pieces.
3. Place, seam side down, 2 in. apart on greased baking sheets. Bake at 375° for 15 minutes or until golden brown.

Monster Curried Cheese Ball

Ice Cream Cone Treats

Bunny Pineapple Smoothies

Ice Cream Cone Treats

I came up with this recipe as a way for my grandkids to enjoy a pre-dinner goody without getting sticky hands. You can also pack the cereal mixture into paper cups and insert a freezer pop stick to form snackable suckers.

—MABEL NOLAN VANCOUVER, WA

START TO FINISH: 15 MIN.
MAKES: 12 SERVINGS

    Colored sprinkles
4 **cups miniature marshmallows**
3 **tablespoons butter**
6 **cups crisp rice cereal**
12 **ice cream cones**

1. Place the sprinkles in a shallow bowl. In a microwave or in a large saucepan over low heat, melt the marshmallows and butter. Remove from heat; stir in cereal.

2. Using greased hands, shape cereal mixture into 12 balls. Pack each ball into an ice cream cone. Dip tops in the sprinkles.

Bunny Pineapple Smoothies

After trying these bunny-topped smoothies, you'll want to hop back for extra servings. Made with orange juice, pineapple sherbet and pina colada yogurt, it'll add a tropical punch to your meals.

—TASTE OF HOME TEST KITCHEN

START TO FINISH: 15 MIN.
MAKES: 10 SERVINGS

2 **cups orange juice**
2 **pints pineapple sherbet**
4 **cups (32 ounces) pina colada yogurt**
4 **medium bananas, quartered**
1 **cup milk**
1 **teaspoon vanilla extract**
2 **cups whipped topping, divided**
1 **drop red food coloring**

1. In a blender, combine half of the orange juice, sherbet, yogurt, bananas, milk and vanilla; cover and process until smooth. Pour into five chilled glasses. Repeat.

2. Place 1½ cups whipped topping in a pastry or plastic bag; cut a medium hole in a corner of the bag. Pipe a bunny face onto each smoothie.

3. Tint remaining whipped topping with food coloring; place in another bag. Cut a small hole in a corner of the bag. Pipe eyes, nose and inside of ears on each bunny face. Beginning from the nose, gently pull a toothpick through the whipped topping toward the edge of the glass to form whiskers. Serve immediately.

Lunch on a Stick

Scooter Snacks

Let the kids help you construct this recipe. The nutritious scooter treats can rev up homework efforts—or tide the kids over till suppertime.

—**DIDI DESJARDINS** DARTMOUTH, MA

START TO FINISH: 30 MIN.
MAKES: 2 SCOOTERS

- 8 slices zucchini (¼ inch thick)
- 6 pretzel sticks, divided
- 2 pieces string cheese (1 ounce each)
- 2 pretzel rods, cut into 3-inch pieces
- 2 tablespoons spreadable garden vegetable cream cheese
- 4 cherry tomatoes, halved
- 2 pimiento-stuffed olives, halved

1. For each of four axles, thread two zucchini slices through a pretzel stick, leaving a 1-in. space in the center. For each scooter, position string cheese between two axles.
2. Attach a pretzel rod with cream cheese to each scooter; top each with a pretzel stick for handlebars. Attach tomato hubcaps and olive headlights and taillights with cream cheese.

Scooter Snacks

Lunch on a Stick

You can use a cookie cutter to cut the cheese slices into shapes. These are great for lunch but make easy appetizers, too.

—**SARA MARTIN** BROOKFIELD, WI

START TO FINISH: 15 MIN.
MAKES: VARIES

- Block of cheddar or Colby-Monterey Jack cheese
- Cooked tortellini
- Wooden skewers (5 to 6 inches)
- Grape tomatoes
- Whole wheat bread slices, cut into 1-inch pieces
- Leaf lettuce, optional
- Sliced deli ham, cut into 1-inch strips
- Seedless red or green grapes

Cut cheese into ¼-in. slices and then into 1-in. pieces. (Smaller pieces may break when threaded on the skewer.)

MAC & CHEESE ON A STICK
Alternately thread cheese slices and tortellini on a skewer. Add grape tomatoes if desired.

HAM & CHEESE ON A STICK *Thread bread, lettuce if desired, cheese and a ribbon of ham on a skewer. Add additional cheese and bread pieces. Hold in place with a grape or grape tomato on each end.*

FRUIT & CHEESE ON A STICK
Alternately thread grapes and cheese on a skewer.

CREATE YOUR OWN LUNCH ON A STICK *Let children place their favorite ingredients on a stick.*

Fruit Salsa with Cinnamon Chips

I first made this fresh, fruity salsa for a family get-together. Now, someone makes it for just about every gathering!

—**JESSICA ROBINSON** INDIAN TRAIL, NC

START TO FINISH: 30 MIN.
MAKES: 2½ CUPS SALSA (80 CHIPS)

- 1 **cup finely chopped fresh strawberries**
- 1 **medium navel orange, peeled and finely chopped**
- 3 **medium kiwifruit, peeled and finely chopped**
- 1 **can (8 ounces) unsweetened crushed pineapple, drained**
- 1 **tablespoon lemon juice**
- 1½ **teaspoons sugar**

CINNAMON CHIPS

- 10 **flour tortillas (8 inches)**
- ¼ **cup butter, melted**
- ⅓ **cup sugar**
- 1 **teaspoon ground cinnamon**

1. In a small bowl, combine the first six ingredients. Cover and refrigerate until serving.

2. For chips, brush tortillas with butter; cut each into eight wedges. Combine sugar and cinnamon; sprinkle over tortillas. Place on ungreased baking sheets.

3. Bake at 350° for 5-10 minutes or just until crisp. Serve with fruit salsa.

DID YOU KNOW?

All you need to make fast work of peeling a kiwifruit is a teaspoon and a ripe—but not too soft—kiwi. First, cut off both ends of the kiwi. Then slip the teaspoon just under the skin, matching the spoon's curve to the curve of the fruit. Now slide the spoon around the kiwi to separate the fruit from the skin, being careful not to dig the spoon into the flesh. Once the spoon has been completely run around the fruit, the kiwifruit will easily slip out of the skin in one smooth piece.

Fruit Salsa with Cinnamon Chips

Rise & Shine Breakfasts

Good morning! Start your day the right way, by digging in to a deliciously easy-to-prepare breakfast. Send your family out the door with smiles and full bellies!

First-Prize Doughnuts

Mini-Chip Cocoa Pancakes

Get your chocolate fix early by whipping up a batch of hot cocoa pancakes dotted with mini chocolate chips. Yum!

—**JOYCE MOYNIHAN** LAKEVILLE, MN

START TO FINISH: 30 MIN.
MAKES: 4 SERVINGS

- 1¼ cups all-purpose flour
- ¼ cup baking cocoa
- ¼ cup sugar
- 3 teaspoons baking powder
- ½ teaspoon salt
- 2 eggs
- 1 cup 2% milk
- 3 tablespoons butter, melted
- 1½ teaspoons vanilla extract
- ⅔ cup miniature semisweet chocolate chips
  Powdered sugar and whipped cream, optional

1. In a large bowl, whisk the first five ingredients. In another bowl, whisk eggs, milk, butter and vanilla until blended. Add to the flour mixture; stir just until moistened. Fold in the chocolate chips.

2. Coat a griddle with cooking spray; heat over medium heat. Pour batter by ¼ cupfuls onto griddle. Cook until bubbles on top begin to pop. Turn; cook until second side is lightly browned. If desired, dust with powdered sugar and serve with whipped cream.

First-Prize Doughnuts

One year I entered 18 different baked goods in the county fair and all of them won ribbons. Here is my favorite prizewinning doughnut recipe. Have fun dressing them up.

—**BETTY CLAYCOMB** ALVERTON, PA

PREP: 25 MIN. + RISING
COOK: 5 MIN./BATCH
MAKES: 20 DOUGHNUTS

- 2 packages (¼ ounce each) active dry yeast
- ½ cup warm water (110° to 115°)
- ½ cup warm 2% milk (110° to 115°)
- ½ cup sugar
- ½ cup shortening
- 2 eggs
- 1 teaspoon salt
- 4½ to 5 cups all-purpose flour
  Oil for deep-fat frying

TOPPINGS

- 1¼ cups confectioners' sugar
- 4 to 6 tablespoons water
  Colored sprinkles and/or assorted breakfast cereals

1. In a large bowl, dissolve yeast in warm water. Add the milk, sugar, shortening, eggs, salt and 2 cups flour; beat until smooth. Stir in enough remaining flour to form a soft dough.

2. Turn onto a floured surface; knead until smooth and elastic, about 6-8 minutes. Place in a greased bowl, turning once to grease the top. Cover and let rise in a warm place until doubled, about 1 hour.

3. Punch dough down. Turn onto a floured surface; roll out to ½-in. thickness. Cut with a floured 2½-in. doughnut cutter. Place on greased baking sheets. Cover and let rise until doubled, about 1 hour.

4. In an electric skillet or deep fryer, heat oil to 375°. Fry doughnuts, a few at a time, until golden brown on both sides. Drain on paper towels.

5. In a shallow bowl, combine confectioners' sugar and water until smooth. Dip warm doughnuts in glaze; decorate as desired with sprinkles and/or cereals.

Mini-Chip Cocoa Pancakes

Toad in the Hole

When my children were learning to cook, this is one of the first recipes I had them prepare. My "little ones" are now grown and have advanced to more difficult recipes, but this continues to be a standby in my home and theirs.

—RUTH LECHLEITER BRECKENRIDGE, MN

START TO FINISH: 15 MIN.
MAKES: 1 SERVING

- 1 **slice of bread**
- 1 **teaspoon butter**
- 1 **egg**
  Salt and pepper to taste

1. Cut a 3-in. hole in the middle of the bread and discard. In a small skillet, melt the butter; place the bread in the skillet.

2. Place egg in the hole. Cook for about 2 minutes over medium heat until the bread is lightly browned. Turn and cook the other side until egg yolk is almost set. Season with salt and pepper.

PILGRIM DOUGHNUT SHIPS

Cut a sail out of paper. Bend it vertically and make two small slits. Thread a pretzel stick "mast" through the slits and push the pretzel into the inner edge of a mini doughnut. Cut a triangle flag out of strawberry Fruit by the Foot and wrap it around the pretzel. Then eat it all up, except the paper!

—NORENE COX EDMONDS, WA

Readers of Norene's blog adore these crafty sea-cruisers. **partypinching.com**

Toad in the Hole

Jolly Jelly Doughnuts

Jolly Jelly Doughnuts

Plump and filled with jelly, these sugar-coated doughnuts will disappear as fast as you can make them.

—**LEE BREMSON** KANSAS CITY, MO

PREP: 25 MIN. + RISING • **COOK:** 30 MIN.
MAKES: ABOUT 2½ DOZEN

- 2 **packages (¼ ounce each) active dry yeast**
- 2 **cups warm milk (110° to 115°)**
- 7 **cups all-purpose flour**
- 4 **egg yolks**
- 1 **egg**
- ½ **cup sugar**
- 1 **teaspoon salt**
- 2 **teaspoons grated lemon peel**
- ½ **teaspoon vanilla extract**
- ½ **cup butter, melted**
  Oil for deep-fat frying
  Red jelly of your choice
  Additional sugar

1. In a large bowl, dissolve the yeast in warm milk. Add 2 cups flour; mix well. Let stand in a warm place for 30 minutes. Add the egg yolks, egg, sugar, salt, lemon peel and vanilla; mix well. Beat in butter and remaining flour. Do not knead. Cover and let rise in a warm place until doubled, about 45 minutes.

2. Punch dough down. On a lightly floured surface, roll out to ½-in. thickness. Cut with a 2½-in. biscuit cutter. Place on lightly greased baking sheets. Cover and let rise until nearly doubled, about 35 minutes.

3. In a deep-fat fryer or electric skillet, heat oil to 375°. Fry doughnuts, a few at a time, for 1½ to 2 minutes on each side or until browned. Drain on paper towels.

4. Cool for 2-3 minutes; cut a small slit with a sharp knife on one side of each doughnut. Cut a small hole in the corner of a pastry or plastic bag; insert a very small round tip. Fill with jelly. Fill each doughnut with about 1 teaspoon jelly. Carefully roll warm doughnuts in sugar. Serve warm.

Fruit Salad Cups

I've been serving this fruit salad for breakfast and brunch for years. The peach pie filing makes it irresistible, and serving it in waffle cones just adds to the fun. Kids especially love it.

—**JUDY HORTON** FORT WORTH, TX

PREP: 20 MIN. + CHILLING
MAKES: 12 SERVINGS

- 1 **can (21 ounces) peach pie filling**
- 2 **cups fresh strawberries, halved**
- 2 **cups green grapes, halved**
- 2 **cups cubed fresh pineapple**
- 3 **medium kiwifruit, peeled, halved and sliced**
- 2 **medium bananas, sliced**
- 1 **can (15 ounces) mandarin oranges, drained**
- 1 **jar (6 ounces) maraschino cherries, drained and halved**
- 12 **ice cream waffle bowls or cones**
- ¼ **cup chopped walnuts, toasted**
  Mint sprigs, optional

1. In a large bowl, combine the first eight ingredients. Refrigerate until serving.

2. Just before serving, spoon salad into waffle bowls and sprinkle with walnuts. Garnish with mint sprigs if desired.

Fruit Salad Cups

Puppy Dog Pancakes

½ cup plus 1 tablespoon sugar, divided
5 teaspoons cornstarch
½ teaspoon ground cinnamon
¼ teaspoon ground nutmeg
2 teaspoons lemon juice
12 slices day-old bread
3 eggs
⅔ cup milk
2 teaspoons vanilla extract
Confectioners' sugar, optional

1. In a large saucepan, cook apples and water over medium heat for 10 minutes or until apples are tender. Combine ½ cup sugar, cornstarch, cinnamon and nutmeg; stir into apple mixture. Bring to a boil; cook and stir for 2 minutes or until thickened. Remove from the heat; stir in the lemon juice.

2. Spread six slices of bread with ⅓ cup filling; top with remaining bread. In a shallow bowl, beat eggs, milk, vanilla and remaining sugar.

3. Dip sandwiches in egg mixture. Cook on a lightly greased hot griddle until golden brown on both sides. Sprinkle with confectioners' sugar if desired.

Apple Pie Sandwiches

Puppy Dog Pancakes

Woof woof! Make breakfast extra special when you set out these puppy pancakes.
—*TASTE OF HOME* TEST KITCHEN

START TO FINISH: 25 MIN.
MAKES: 4 SERVINGS

1 **cup all-purpose flour**
1 **teaspoon sugar**
¾ **teaspoon baking powder**
½ **teaspoon salt**
1 **egg**
1 **cup buttermilk**
1 **tablespoon butter, melted**
1 **tablespoon chocolate syrup**
2 **drops strawberry syrup**
8 **semisweet chocolate chips**

1. In a large bowl, combine flour, sugar, baking powder and salt. In another large bowl, whisk the egg, buttermilk and butter. Stir into the dry ingredients just until moistened. Place ⅔ cup of the batter in a small bowl; stir in the chocolate syrup. Place 1 teaspoon of batter in another bowl; stir in strawberry syrup.

2. For puppy ears, pour eight 1 tablespoonfuls of the chocolate batter onto a lightly greased large hot griddle. For muzzle and eyes, spoon eight 1 teaspoonfuls and eight ¼ teaspoonfuls of chocolate batter onto the griddle. For tongues, spoon four ⅛ teaspoonfuls of pink batter onto the griddle. Turn when bubbles form on top of pancakes; cook until the second side is golden brown. Repeat for plain pancakes, pouring batter by ¼ cupfuls onto griddle.

3. To assemble, arrange ears, eyes, muzzle and tongue on plain pancakes; top eyes with chocolate chips.

Apple Pie Sandwiches

We usually enjoy these sandwiches for breakfast, but they're also just as good for lunch or even dessert.
—**GLORIA JARRETT** LOVELAND, OH

START TO FINISH: 30 MIN.
MAKES: 6 SERVINGS

2 **cups diced peeled tart apples**
1 **cup water**

Best Scrambled Eggs

They don't call them "the best scrambled eggs" for nothing. Some people don't typically love scrambled eggs, but once they try these, they're hooked for life.

—**LAURIE TIETZE** LONGVIEW, TX

START TO FINISH: 20 MIN.
MAKES: 4 SERVINGS

- 8 **eggs**
- 5 **slices process American cheese, chopped**
- ¼ **cup cubed fully cooked ham**
- ¼ **cup 2% milk**
- 1 **tablespoon spicy brown mustard**
- ⅛ **teaspoon salt**
- ⅛ **teaspoon pepper**

Heat a nonstick skillet coated with cooking spray over medium heat. Whisk all the ingredients; add to skillet. Cook and stir until set.

Peanut Butter & Banana Waffles

These are a refreshing change from your everyday waffles. I like to make big batches so I can freeze the leftovers and reheat them later for a quick breakfast.

—**CHRISTINA ADDISON** BLANCHESTER, OH

PREP: 10 MIN. • **COOK:** 5 MIN./BATCH
MAKES: 16 WAFFLES

- 1¾ **cups all-purpose flour**
- 2 **tablespoons sugar**
- 3 **teaspoons baking powder**
- ¼ **teaspoon salt**
- ¾ **cup creamy peanut butter**
- ½ **cup canola oil**
- 2 **eggs**
- 1¾ **cups 2% milk**
- 1 **cup mashed ripe bananas (about 2 medium)**

1. In a large bowl, whisk flour, sugar, baking powder and salt. Place peanut butter in another bowl; gradually whisk in oil. Whisk in eggs and milk. Add to dry ingredients; stir just until moistened. Stir in bananas.

2. Bake in a preheated waffle iron according to manufacturer's directions until golden brown.

FREEZE OPTION *Cool waffles on wire racks. Freeze between layers of waxed paper in resealable plastic freezer bags. Reheat waffles in a toaster on medium*

Best Scrambled Eggs

setting. Or, microwave each waffle on high for 30-60 seconds or until heated through.

Peach & Sausage Breakfast Squares

The ingredients may sound unusual, but trust me, this breakfast bake is really tasty. Sausage, sweet peaches and pancake mix come together for a complete meal.

—**JUDITH BOWDEN** SANFORD, NC

PREP: 15 MIN. • **BAKE:** 30 MIN.
MAKES: 6 SERVINGS

- 1 **can (15¼ ounces) sliced peaches**
- ¼ **cup sugar**
- 1 **tablespoon cornstarch**
- ¾ **cup maple syrup**
- 1 **tablespoon butter**
- 2 **cups pancake mix**
- 1 **egg, beaten**
- 2 **tablespoons canola oil**

- 1 **package (7 ounces) frozen fully cooked breakfast sausage links, thawed and halved lengthwise**

1. Drain peaches, reserving juice; set aside. In a small saucepan, combine sugar and cornstarch; stir in ½ cup reserved peach juice until smooth. Bring to a boil. Cook and stir for 1-2 minutes or until thickened. Stir in syrup and butter; set aside and keep warm.

2. Combine the remaining juice and enough water to measure 1 cup. In a small bowl, combine the pancake mix, egg, oil and juice mixture. Pour into a greased 13x9-in. baking dish. Arrange sausages and peaches over the top.

3. Bake, uncovered, at 350° for 30-40 minutes or until a toothpick inserted near the center comes out clean. Cut into squares; serve squares warm with peach syrup.

Berry Breakfast
Parfaits

Cinnamon Flapjacks

Berry Breakfast Parfaits

Expecting brunch company, but short on time? Parfaits are the perfect solution. Feel free to mix and match with whatever berries you have on hand.
—**LISA SPEER** PALM BEACH, FL

START TO FINISH: 20 MIN.
MAKES: 8 SERVINGS

- 6½ cups frozen unsweetened raspberries
- ¼ cup packed brown sugar
- ¼ cup orange juice
- 2 tablespoons cornstarch
- ½ teaspoon grated orange peel
- 2 cups fresh blueberries
- 2 cups fresh blackberries
- 2 cups granola
- 4 cups vanilla Greek yogurt
  Additional brown sugar, optional

1. Place the raspberries and brown sugar in a blender; cover and process until pureed. Press through a sieve; discard seeds.

2. In a small saucepan, combine raspberry puree, orange juice, cornstarch and orange peel. Cook and stir over medium heat until thickened and bubbly. Reduce heat to low; cook and stir 2 minutes longer. Remove from the heat; cool.

3. In eight parfait glasses, layer half the raspberry sauce, berries, granola and yogurt. Repeat layers. Sprinkle with additional brown sugar if desired. Serve immediately.

Cinnamon Flapjacks

Kids will love helping make this breakfast treat for Dad. You can also change the letter shapes for any occasion, especially Mother's Day. Don't forget to serve the homemade syrup on the side.
—*TASTE OF HOME* TEST KITCHEN

PREP: 15 MIN. • **COOK:** 5 MIN./BATCH
MAKES: 4 SERVINGS (¾ CUP SYRUP)

- 2 cups complete buttermilk pancake mix
- 1½ cups water
- 1 tablespoon maple syrup
- 1 tablespoon butter, melted
- ½ teaspoon ground cinnamon
SYRUP
- 1 cup packed brown sugar
- ¼ cup water
- 1 tablespoon butter
- ½ teaspoon vanilla extract

1. In a bowl, combine pancake mix, water, syrup, butter and cinnamon. Pour batter into a plastic squirt bottle. Squeeze batter into desired letters and shapes onto a greased hot griddle. When underside is browned, turn pancakes and cook until second side is golden brown.

2. Meanwhile, in a small saucepan, combine the brown sugar, water and butter. Bring to a boil. Reduce heat; simmer, uncovered, for 4-5 minutes or until sugar is dissolved. Remove from the heat; stir in vanilla. Serve with flapjacks.

Apple-Raisin Baked Oatmeal

I often whip up this recipe for our seven children. It's inexpensive to put on the table, and the kids always enjoy the fun fruit toppings.

—**CHRISTINA SMEAL** FAIRMONT, WV

PREP: 20 MIN. • **BAKE:** 35 MIN.
MAKES: 6 SERVINGS

- 3 **cups old-fashioned oats**
- ½ **cup packed brown sugar**
- 2 **teaspoons baking powder**
- 1½ **teaspoons ground cinnamon**
- ½ **teaspoon salt**
- ⅛ **teaspoon ground nutmeg**
- 2 **eggs**
- 2 **cups fat-free milk**
- 1 **medium apple, chopped**
- ⅓ **cup raisins**
- ⅓ **cup chopped walnuts**
  Additional fat-free milk and
  fruit toppings, optional

1. Preheat oven to 350°. In a large bowl, combine the first six ingredients. Whisk eggs and milk; stir into the dry ingredients until blended. Let stand 5 minutes. Stir in the apple, raisins and walnuts.

2. Transfer to an 8-in.-square baking dish coated with cooking spray. Bake, uncovered, 35-40 minutes or until edges are lightly browned and a thermometer reads 160°. Serve with additional milk and fruit toppings if desired.

HOW TO

MEASURE NUTS

❶ It's important to know when to chop an ingredient for a recipe. If the word "chopped" comes before an ingredient when listed in a recipe, then you should chop the ingredient before measuring. If the word "chopped" is listed after the ingredient, you should measure first, then chop.

❷ This recipe calls for chopped walnuts, so be sure to chop them before measuring.

Apple-Raisin
Baked Oatmeal

Ham and Cheese Stratas

Breakfast Wraps

We like quick and simple morning meals during the week. These wraps can be prepped ahead of time and then warmed up for just a minute in the microwave.

—**BETTY KLEBERGER** FLORISSANT, MO

START TO FINISH: 15 MIN.
MAKES: 4 SERVINGS

- 6 eggs
- 2 tablespoons milk
- ¼ teaspoon pepper
- 1 tablespoon canola oil
- 1 cup (4 ounces) shredded cheddar cheese
- ¾ cup diced fully cooked ham
- 4 flour tortillas (8 inches), warmed

1. In a small bowl, whisk the eggs, milk and pepper. In a large skillet, heat oil. Add egg mixture; cook and stir over medium heat until eggs are completely set. Stir in cheese and ham.

2. Spoon egg mixture down the center of each tortilla; roll up.

FREEZE OPTION *Wrap cooled egg wrap in plastic wrap and freeze in a resealable plastic bag for up to 1 month. To use, thaw in refrigerator overnight. Remove plastic wrap; wrap tortilla in a moist paper towel. Microwave on high for 30-60 seconds or until heated through. Serve immediately.*

Breakfast Wraps

Ham and Cheese Stratas

Almost too cute to eat, these mini egg bakes make a handy portable meal. Even with a creamy texture, they hold their shape and have the perfect amount of mix-ins.

—**SHIRLEY WARREN** THIENSVILLE, WI

PREP: 20 MIN. • **BAKE:** 25 MIN.
MAKES: 1 DOZEN

- 1 small onion, chopped
- 1 teaspoon canola oil
- 5 eggs
- 1½ cups 2% milk
- 1 cup (4 ounces) shredded cheddar cheese
- 2 teaspoons Dijon mustard
- ¼ teaspoon salt
- ⅛ teaspoon pepper
- 3 cups cubed day-old Italian bread (½-inch cubes)
- 1 cup cubed fully cooked ham
- 1 plum tomato, seeded and chopped

1. Preheat oven to 350°. In a small skillet, saute onion in oil until tender. In a large bowl, whisk eggs, milk, cheese, mustard, salt and pepper. Stir in bread cubes, ham, tomato and onion.

2. Spoon into greased or foil-lined muffin cups. Bake, uncovered, 22-26 minutes or until a knife inserted near center comes out clean.

DID YOU KNOW?

When a recipe calls for canola oil, vegetable oil can be substituted in equal amounts. There should be no difference in the final result for a recipe.

Nutty Waffle Sandwiches

Pigs in a Pool

My kids love sausage and pancakes, but making them for breakfast during the busy week was out of the question. My version of pigs-in-a-blanket is a fine alternative to the frozen, packaged kind.

—**LISA DODD** GREENVILLE, SC

PREP: 45 MIN. • **BAKE:** 20 MIN.
MAKES: 12 SERVINGS

- 1 **pound reduced-fat bulk pork sausage**
- 2 **cups all-purpose flour**
- ¼ **cup sugar**
- 1 **tablespoon baking powder**
- 1 **teaspoon salt**
- ½ **teaspoon ground cinnamon**
- ¼ **teaspoon ground nutmeg**
- 1 **egg, lightly beaten**
- 2 **cups fat-free milk**
- 2 **tablespoons canola oil**
- 2 **tablespoons honey**
  Maple syrup, optional

1. Preheat oven to 350°. Coat mini-muffin cups with cooking spray. Shape sausage into forty-eight ¾-in. balls. Place meatballs on a rack coated with cooking spray in a shallow baking pan. Bake 15-20 minutes or until cooked through. Drain on paper towels. In a large bowl, whisk flour, sugar, baking powder, salt and spices. In another bowl, whisk egg, milk, oil and honey until blended. Add to flour mixture; stir just until moistened.

2. Place a sausage ball into each mini-muffin cup; cover with batter. Bake 20-25 minutes or until lightly browned. Cool 5 minutes before removing from pans to wire racks. Serve warm with syrup if desired.

FREEZE OPTION *Freeze cooled muffins in resealable plastic freezer bags. To use, microwave each muffin on high for 20-30 seconds or until heated through.*

NOTE *This recipe was tested in a 1,100-watt microwave.*

Nutty Waffle Sandwiches

You can't go wrong with peanut butter and Nutella, but the secret here is using really juicy strawberries. Never tried Nutella? Look for the hazelnut-flavored spread near the peanut butter at the grocery store. Little ones won't be able to resist digging in to this easy-to-make breakfast sandwich.

—**FRANCES PIETSCH** FLOWER MOUND, TX

START TO FINISH: 15 MIN.
MAKES: 4 SERVINGS

- 8 **frozen multigrain waffles**
- ½ **cup Nutella**
- 2 **medium bananas, sliced**
- 1 **cup sliced fresh strawberries**
- ½ **cup peanut butter**

Toast waffles according to package directions. Spread four waffles with Nutella. Layer with bananas and strawberries. Spread remaining waffles with peanut butter; place over top.

Orange Fruit Cups

Eating fruit out of a fruit bowl is a unique way to start the day. The kids will have fun filling them up.

—**SUZAN L. WIENER** SPRING HILL, FL

START TO FINISH: 20 MIN.
MAKES: 4 SERVINGS

- 2 **medium navel oranges, halved**
- 1 **small apple, chopped**
- 1 **small banana, sliced**
- ¼ **cup plain yogurt**
- ¼ **teaspoon ground cinnamon**
  Additional ground cinnamon, optional

1. Using a paring or grapefruit knife and a spoon, scoop out pulp from oranges, leaving a shell. Separate orange sections and chop; transfer to a small bowl.

2. Add the apple, banana, yogurt and cinnamon. Fill orange shells with fruit mixture. Sprinkle with additional cinnamon if desired. Serve cups immediately.

French Toast Sticks

French Toast Sticks

Keep these French toast sticks in the freezer for an instant morning start. The convenient size makes them a great buffet item.

—*TASTE OF HOME* TEST KITCHEN

PREP: 20 MIN. + FREEZING • **BAKE:** 20 MIN.
MAKES: 1½ DOZEN

- 6 **slices day-old Texas toast**
- 4 **eggs**
- 1 **cup milk**
- 2 **tablespoons sugar**
- 1 **teaspoon vanilla extract**
- ¼ **to ½ teaspoon ground cinnamon**
- 1 **cup crushed cornflakes, optional**
  Confectioners' sugar, optional
  Maple syrup

1. Cut each piece of bread into thirds; place in an ungreased 13x9-in. dish. In a large bowl, whisk the eggs, milk, sugar, vanilla and cinnamon. Pour over bread; soak 2 minutes, turning once. Coat bread with the cornflake crumbs on all sides if desired.

2. Place in a greased 15x10x1-in. baking pan. Freeze sticks until firm, about 45 minutes. Transfer to an airtight container or resealable freezer bag and store in the freezer.

TO USE FROZEN FRENCH TOAST STICKS *Place desired number of sticks on a greased baking sheet. Bake at 425° for 8 minutes. Turn; bake 10-12 minutes longer or until golden brown. Sprinkle with confectioners' sugar if desired. Serve with syrup.*

TOP TIP

Instead of just milk, I sometimes add flavored liquid coffee creamer with a touch of milk to the eggs when making French toast. It tastes so good, you might not even need syrup!
—**KAREN M.** HAMPTON, VA

Banana Pancake Snowmen

Baked Long Johns

Banana Pancake Snowmen

You'll be saying "Let it snow!" when you see these yummy pancakes shaped like snowmen. The kids can decorate their own with pretzel sticks for arms and chocolate chips, raisins or cranberries for faces and buttons.

—PHYLLIS SCHMALZ KANSAS CITY, KS

PREP: 15 MIN. • **COOK:** 5 MIN./BATCH
MAKES: 7 SNOWMEN

- 1 **cup complete buttermilk pancake mix**
- ¾ **cup water**
- ⅓ **cup mashed ripe banana**
- 1 **teaspoon confectioners' sugar**
  Optional toppings: pretzel sticks, chocolate chips, dried cranberries and/or halved banana slices

1. In a small bowl, stir the pancake mix, water and banana just until moistened.

2. Pour ¼ cup batter onto a greased hot griddle, making three circles to form a snowman. Turn when bubbles form on top. Cook until second side is golden brown. Transfer to a serving plate. Repeat with remaining batter.

3. Sprinkle with confectioners' sugar. Decorate the snowmen with pretzels, chocolate chips, cranberries and/or banana if desired.

Baked Long Johns

These doughnuts are baked instead of fried, so you'll feel a little less guilty.

—NICKI LAZORIK MELLEN, WI

PREP: 15 MIN. • **BAKE:** 20 MIN. + COOLING
MAKES: 8 SERVINGS

- 2 **cups all-purpose flour**
- ½ **cup sugar**
- 2 **teaspoons baking powder**
- ½ **teaspoon salt**
- ¼ **teaspoon ground cinnamon**
- 2 **eggs**
- ¾ **cup fat-free milk**
- 1 **tablespoon butter, melted**
- 1 **teaspoon vanilla extract**
GLAZE
- ¾ **cup semisweet chocolate chips**
- 1 **tablespoon butter**
- 4½ **teaspoons fat-free milk**

1. In a small bowl, combine flour, sugar, baking powder, salt and cinnamon. In another bowl, whisk the eggs, milk, butter and vanilla. Stir into dry ingredients just until moistened.

2. Transfer to eight 4½ x 2½ x 1½-in. loaf pans coated with cooking spray. Bake at 325° for 18-22 minutes or until golden brown. Immediately remove from pans to a wire rack to cool completely.

3. In a microwave, melt chocolate chips and butter. Add milk; stir until smooth. Dip tops of doughnuts in glaze. Return to wire rack; let stand until set.

Main Dishes for the Family

Even the pickiest of eaters will be enticed by these tasty and appealing meals. Fun twists on mealtime favorites delight kids and adults alike.

Homemade Fish Sticks

Hot Dog Speed Racer

Homemade Fish Sticks

I'm a native of Maine with English ancestry, and I've gotta have my fish and chips. I'm also a nutritionist, so I came up with this better-for-you baked version.
—**JENNIFER ROWLAND** ELIZABETHTOWN, KY

START TO FINISH: 25 MIN.
MAKES: 2 SERVINGS

- ½ **cup dry bread crumbs**
- ½ **teaspoon salt**
- ½ **teaspoon paprika**
- ½ **teaspoon lemon-pepper seasoning**
- ½ **cup all-purpose flour**
- 1 **egg, beaten**
- ¾ **pound cod fillets, cut into 1-inch strips**
  Butter-flavored cooking spray

1. Preheat oven to 400°. In a shallow bowl, mix bread crumbs and seasonings. Place flour and egg in separate shallow bowls. Dip fish in flour to coat both sides; shake off excess. Dip in egg, then in the crumb mixture, patting to help coating adhere.

2. Place on a baking sheet coated with cooking spray; spritz with butter-flavored cooking spray. Bake 10-12 minutes or until fish just begins to flake easily with a fork, turning once.

Hot Dog Speed Racer

Getting a little creative with food can make meals more appealing for children, and a lot easier for parents. A Hot Dog Speed Racer is sure to zoom off the plate!
—**JENNI SHARP** MILWAUKEE, WI

START TO FINISH: 15 MIN.
MAKES: 1 SERVING

- 1 **hot dog bun, split**
- 6 **pretzel sticks, divided**
- 4 **sweet pickle slices**
- 4 **slices ripe olives**
- 2 **hot dogs, cooked, divided**
- 1 **miniature pretzel**
- 1 **teaspoon prepared mustard**
- ½ **colossal ripe olive**
- 2 **slices miniature pepperoni**

1. Place bun on a plate, cut side up. For each wheel, insert a pretzel stick partway into bun; attach a pickle and olive slice.

2. Cut a slit 1 in. from the end of a hot dog; insert miniature pretzel for steering wheel. Place in bun.

3. Cut remaining hot dog in half for the driver (save remaining half for another use); insert a pretzel stick halfway into the cut end.

4. Place mustard in a food-safe plastic bag; cut a small hole in a corner of bag. Pipe face onto driver. Insert driver behind steering wheel. Place olive half on driver for helmet.

5. Break remaining pretzel stick in half; place on steering wheel for the arms. Using mustard, attach pepperoni slices for headlights. Serve immediately.

Muffin Tin Pizzas

Soon after we baked these mini pizzas, my kids were already requesting more. The no-cook pizza sauce and refrigerated dough make this meal a snap.

—MELISSA HAINES VALPARAISO, IN

PREP: 25 MIN. • **BAKE:** 10 MIN.
MAKES: 8 SERVINGS

- 1 **can (15 ounces) tomato sauce**
- 1 **can (6 ounces) tomato paste**
- 1 **teaspoon dried basil**
- ½ **teaspoon garlic salt**
- ¼ **teaspoon onion powder**
- ¼ **teaspoon sugar**
- 1 **tube (11 ounces) refrigerated thin pizza crust**
- 1½ **cups (6 ounces) shredded part-skim mozzarella cheese**
- ½ **cup finely chopped fresh mushrooms**
- ½ **cup finely chopped fresh broccoli**
- 16 **slices pepperoni, halved**

1. Preheat oven to 425°. In a small bowl, mix the first six ingredients.
2. Unroll pizza crust; cut into 16 squares. Press the squares onto bottom and up sides of 16 ungreased muffin cups, allowing the corners to hang over edge.
3. Spoon 1 tablespoon sauce mixture into each cup. Top with the cheese, mushrooms, broccoli and pepperoni. Bake 10-12 minutes or until crust is golden brown. Serve the remaining sauce mixture, warmed if desired, with pizzas.

DID YOU KNOW?

Onion and garlic powders tend to absorb moisture from the air, especially when it's warmer outside. Store these powders in airtight spice jars to keep them free from humidity.

Muffin Tin Pizzas

**Bacon & Cheese
Meatball Sliders**

Bacon & Cheese Meatball Sliders

These meatball sliders are a party-on-a-stick. All you have to do is add mustard, ketchup or barbecue sauce to the table for a dipping good time.

—TASTE OF HOME TEST KITCHEN

PREP: 50 MIN. + STANDING • **GRILL:** 10 MIN.
MAKES: 6 SERVINGS

- 12 **frozen bread dough dinner rolls**
- 1 **egg**
- 1 **teaspoon water**
- 1 **tablespoon sesame seeds**

KABOBS

- ¾ **cup seasoned bread crumbs**
- 6 **bacon strips, cooked and crumbled**
- 2 **eggs, lightly beaten**
- 1½ **teaspoons Worcestershire sauce**
- ½ **teaspoon garlic salt**
- 1½ **pounds ground sirloin**
- 1 **medium sweet red pepper or green pepper, cut into 1-inch pieces**
- 1 **small red onion, cut into 1-inch pieces**
- 6 **slices process American cheese, cut into quarters**

1. Thaw dough according to package directions. Cut each roll in half; reshape portions into balls. Place 2 in. apart on lightly greased baking sheets. Cover with clean kitchen towels; let rise in a warm place until almost doubled, about 30 minutes.
2. Uncover dough; gently press to flatten slightly. Whisk egg and water; brush over tops. Sprinkle with sesame seeds. Bake at 400° for 8-10 minutes or until golden brown. Remove to wire racks.
3. In a large bowl, combine the first five kabob ingredients. Crumble beef over mixture and mix well. Shape into 24 patties. On 24 metal or soaked wooden skewers, alternately thread the patties, red pepper and onion, inserting patties sideways.
4. Moisten a paper towel with cooking oil; using long-handled tongs, lightly coat the grill rack. Grill kabobs, covered, over medium-high heat for 4-5 minutes on each side or until the patties are no longer pink. Remove from the grill; immediately top patties with cheese. Cut buns in half; assemble sliders.

Coconut-Crusted Turkey Strips

Coconut-Crusted Turkey Strips

My granddaughter shared these baked turkey strips with me. With a plum dipping sauce on the side, they're just the thing for a light dinner.

—AGNES WARD STRATFORD, ON

START TO FINISH: 30 MIN.
MAKES: 6 SERVINGS

- 2 **egg whites**
- 2 **teaspoons sesame oil**
- ½ **cup flaked coconut, toasted**
- ½ **cup dry bread crumbs**
- 2 **tablespoons sesame seeds, toasted**
- ½ **teaspoon salt**
- 1½ **pounds turkey breast tenderloins, cut into ½-inch strips**
  Cooking spray

DIPPING SAUCE

- ½ **cup plum sauce**
- ⅓ **cup unsweetened pineapple juice**
- 1½ **teaspoons prepared mustard**
- 1 **teaspoon cornstarch**

1. Preheat oven to 425°. In a shallow bowl, whisk egg whites and oil. In another shallow bowl, mix coconut, bread crumbs, sesame seeds and salt. Dip turkey in egg mixture, then in coconut mixture, patting to help coating adhere.
2. Place on baking sheets coated with cooking spray; spritz turkey with cooking spray. Bake 10-12 minutes or until turkey is no longer pink, turning once.
3. Meanwhile, in a small saucepan, mix sauce ingredients. Bring to a boil; cook and stir 1-2 minutes or until thickened. Serve turkey with sauce.
NOTE *To toast coconut, spread in a 15x10x1-in. baking pan. Bake at 350° for 5-10 minutes or until golden brown, stirring frequently.*

Camping Haystacks

Parmesan Chicken Nuggets

My 3-year-old went through a chicken-nuggets-and-French-fries-only stage, so I made these golden nuggets for him. Even the grown-ups liked them!
—AMANDA LIVESAY MOBILE, AL

START TO FINISH: 30 MIN.
MAKES: 8 SERVINGS

- ¼ cup butter, melted
- 1 cup panko (Japanese) bread crumbs
- ½ cup grated Parmesan cheese
- ½ teaspoon kosher salt
- 1½ pounds boneless skinless chicken breasts, cut into 1-inch cubes
  Marinara sauce, optional

1. Place butter in a shallow bowl. Combine the bread crumbs, cheese and salt in another shallow bowl. Dip chicken in butter, then roll in crumbs.
2. Place in a single layer on two 15x10x1-in. baking pans. Bake at 375° for 15-18 minutes or until no longer pink, turning once. Serve with marinara sauce if desired.
FREEZE OPTION *Cool chicken nuggets. Freeze in freezer containers. To use, partially thaw in the refrigerator overnight. Place on a baking sheet and reheat in a preheated 375° oven 7-12 minutes or until heated through.*

Parmesan Chicken Nuggets

Camping Haystacks

Try this layered dish for a satisfying meal after a busy day. We love the combo of canned chili, corn chips and taco toppings.
—GAYLENE ANDERSON SANDY, UT

START TO FINISH: 15 MIN.
MAKES: 2 SERVINGS

- 1 can (15 ounces) chili with beans
- 2 packages (1 ounce each) corn chips
- ½ cup shredded cheddar cheese
- 1½ cups chopped lettuce
- 1 small tomato, chopped
- ½ cup salsa
- 2 tablespoons sliced ripe olives
- 2 tablespoons sour cream

In a small saucepan, heat chili. Divide corn chips between two plates; top with chili. Layer with cheese, lettuce, tomato, salsa, olives and sour cream. Serve immediately.

PBJ on a Stick

Take the classic peanut butter and jelly sandwich on the go. The skewers make easy snacks, and fruit adds to the fun.
—SARA MARTIN BROOKFIELD, WI

START TO FINISH: 10 MIN.
MAKES: 4 SKEWERS

- 2 peanut butter and jelly sandwiches
- 4 wooden skewers (5 to 6 inches)
- 1 cup seedless red or green grapes
- 1 small banana, sliced

Cut sandwiches into 1-in. squares. For each skewer, alternately thread the grapes, sandwich squares and banana slices onto skewers. Serve immediately.

Pizza Tots

Pizza Tots

Tater Tots, pizza sauce, mozzarella and pepperoni—it all adds up to the dinner of a kid's dreams! And I like that it's ready without much fuss.

—ANNIE RUNDLE MUSKEGO, WI

START TO FINISH: 30 MIN.
MAKES: 6 SERVINGS

- 4 **cups frozen miniature Tater Tots**
- ½ **cup pizza sauce**
- 1½ **cups (6 ounces) shredded part-skim mozzarella cheese**
- 12 **slices pepperoni**
- ¼ **teaspoon Italian seasoning Crushed red pepper flakes, optional**

1. Bake Tater Tots according to package directions on a 12-in. pizza pan.
2. Top with pizza sauce, cheese and pepperoni. Sprinkle with Italian seasoning and, if desired, pepper flakes. Bake 5-7 minutes longer or until cheese is melted.

Root Beer Glazed Chicken

My husband tweaked a chicken recipe to suit our tastes, and the result is fabulous. Our young son loves it!

—STACY KOLOJAY STREATOR, IL

START TO FINISH: 30 MIN.
MAKES: 4 SERVINGS

- 4 **boneless skinless chicken breast halves (6 ounces each)**
- 2 **tablespoons canola oil**
- 1 **cup root beer**
- ½ **cup packed brown sugar**
- ¼ **cup ketchup**
- 4 **teaspoons Dijon mustard**
- 2 **teaspoons grated lemon peel**

1. Flatten chicken breasts slightly. In a large skillet, cook chicken in oil for 4-6 minutes on each side or until a thermometer reads 170°. Remove and keep warm.
2. Stir the root beer, brown sugar, ketchup, mustard and lemon peel into the skillet. Bring to a boil. Cook and stir for 6-8 minutes or until thickened. Return chicken to skillet; heat through.

Octopus and Seaweed

Little ones will squirm with delight when they get a look at these remarkable sea creature hot dogs perched on a bed of tasty ramen seaweed.

—KERRY TITTLE LITTLE ROCK, AR

START TO FINISH: 15 MIN.
MAKES: 4 SERVINGS

- 1 **package (3 ounces) beef ramen noodles**
- 4 **hot dogs**
- 5 **drops liquid green food coloring, optional Prepared mustard**

1. In a large saucepan, bring 1½ cups water to a boil. Add the noodles and contents of seasoning packet. Boil for 3-4 minutes or until the noodles are tender.
2. Meanwhile, add 4 in. of water to another large saucepan; bring to a boil. Cut each hot dog lengthwise into eight strips to within 2 in of one end. Drop into the boiling water; cook until heated through.
3. Add food coloring to noodles if desired. Drain if necessary. Place noodles on serving plates; top with a hot dog. Add eyes and mouth with dabs of mustard.

Octopus and Seaweed

Pizza on a Stick

My daughter and her friends had a blast turning sausage, pepperoni, veggies and pizza dough into these cute kabobs.

—CHARLENE WOODS NORFOLK, VA

START TO FINISH: 30 MIN.
MAKES: 5 SERVINGS

- 8 ounces Italian turkey sausage links
- 2 cups whole fresh mushrooms
- 2 cups cherry tomatoes
- 1 medium onion, cut into 1-inch pieces
- 1 large green pepper, cut into 1-inch pieces
- 30 slices turkey pepperoni (2 ounces)
- 1 tube (13.8 ounces) refrigerated pizza crust
- 1½ cups (6 ounces) shredded part-skim mozzarella cheese
- 1¼ cups pizza sauce, warmed

1. Preheat oven to 400°. In a large nonstick skillet, cook sausage over medium heat until no longer pink; drain. When cool enough to handle, cut sausage into 20 pieces. On 10 metal or wooden skewers, alternately thread sausage, vegetables and pepperoni.
2. Unroll pizza dough onto a lightly floured surface; cut widthwise into 1-in.-wide strips. Starting at the pointed end of a prepared skewer, pierce skewer through one end of dough strip. Spiral-wrap dough strip around skewer, allowing vegetables and meats to peek through. Wrap the remaining end of dough strip around skewer above the first ingredient. Repeat with remaining dough strips and prepared skewers.
3. Arrange kabobs on a baking sheet coated with cooking spray. Bake 10-12 minutes or until vegetables are tender and pizza crust is golden. Immediately sprinkle with cheese. Serve with pizza sauce.

Pizza on a Stick

Love You Potpies

With its golden brown crust and scrumptious filling, these delicious potpies will warm you right up. They're the perfect way to show others you care.

—**LAURIE JENSEN** CADILLAC, MI

PREP: 40 MIN. • **BAKE:** 10 MIN.
MAKES: 4 SERVINGS

- 1 sheet refrigerated pie pastry
- 1 egg
- 1 tablespoon heavy whipping cream
- ¼ cup shredded Parmesan cheese, optional

FILLING

- 1 tablespoon butter
- 2 teaspoons olive oil
- 1 medium potato, peeled and cut into ½-inch pieces
- 2 small carrots, cut into ½-inch pieces
- 1 small onion, chopped
- ¼ cup finely chopped celery
- 3 tablespoons all-purpose flour
- 1½ cups chicken broth
- 2 cups cubed cooked chicken (½-inch)
- ⅓ cup frozen peas
- ¼ cup heavy whipping cream
- 2 teaspoons minced fresh parsley
- ½ teaspoon garlic salt
- ⅛ teaspoon pepper

1. Preheat oven to 425°. On a lightly floured surface, unroll pastry sheet. Cut sixteen hearts with a floured 2-in. heart-shaped cookie cutter. Place on an ungreased baking sheet.
2. In a small bowl, whisk egg and cream; brush over hearts. If desired, sprinkle with cheese. Bake 8-10 minutes or until golden brown.
3. For filling, in a large skillet, heat butter and oil over medium-high heat. Add vegetables; cook and stir until tender.
4. Stir in flour until blended; gradually whisk in broth. Bring to a boil, stirring constantly; cook and stir 2 minutes or until thickened. Stir in the remaining ingredients; heat through. Spoon into four 10-oz. ramekins or bowls; top with heart pastries.

Ham 'n' Cheese Spiders

Kids really enjoy eating these creepy spider-shaped sandwiches. It's worth the effort to put them together.

—**KENDRA BARCLAY** DE KALB, IL

PREP: 30 MIN. • **BAKE:** 15 MIN.
MAKES: 5 SANDWICHES

- 1 tube (12 ounces) refrigerated flaky buttermilk biscuits, separated into 10 biscuits
- 1 tube (11 ounces) refrigerated breadsticks, separated into 12 breadsticks
- 1 cup chopped fully cooked ham
- 2 tablespoons finely chopped onion
- 2 tablespoons butter, softened
- 1½ teaspoons prepared mustard
- 5 slices process American cheese
- 1 egg yolk
- 1 teaspoon water
- 2 tablespoons sliced ripe olives
- 1 tablespoon diced pimientos
- 1 teaspoon poppy seeds

1. On two greased baking sheets, pat five biscuits into 3½-in. circles. Cut one breadstick in half lengthwise, then in half widthwise, creating four strips. Repeat nine times (save remaining breadsticks for another use). Position eight strips of dough around each biscuit to resemble spider legs; twist and press lightly onto baking sheet. Tuck a ½-in. foil ball under each dough strip so it stands up in the center of the strip.
2. Combine the ham, onion, butter and mustard; spoon 3 tablespoons onto each biscuit circle. Fold cheese slices into quarters and place over ham mixture. Pat remaining biscuits into 4-in. circles; place over filling. Pinch edges to seal.
3. In a small bowl, beat egg yolk and water. Brush over tops of biscuits and breadsticks. On each spider, position two olive slices for eyes; place the pimientos in center of olives. Sprinkle with poppy seeds. Bake at 375° for 15-20 minutes or until browned.

Ham 'n' Cheese Spiders

Fun Fish Pastries

3. Divide dough into 22 equal pieces. Pat or roll each piece into a 4-in. circle, ¼-in. thick.

4. Place eight circles among two greased baking sheets. Place a heaping tablespoonful of filling in the center of each circle.

5. For fins and tails, cut six circles into fourths. Cut lines into each curved side. Place two fins and a tail on each circle on baking sheets, attaching with water. Press onto circles.

6. In the remaining eight circles, cut scale shapes into bodies using the small end of a pastry bag coupler. Brush edges with water and place over filling; press to seal. Brush tops of pastries with egg white.

7. Bake at 400° for 10-15 minutes or until golden brown. For eyes, cut small circles out of mozzarella using the coupler; place on hot pastries with a piece of olive in the center for pupils. Garnish plates with endive and blueberries if desired.

8. In a small saucepan, combine sauce ingredients. Cook and stir over medium heat until cheese is melted. Serve with pastries.

Taco Salad Waffles

This recipe turns popular Tex-Mex taco salad into a build-your-own main dish. I've also served it as a brunch option.
—**TRISHA KRUSE** EAGLE, ID

START TO FINISH: 25 MIN.
MAKES: 4 SERVINGS

- 1 **pound ground beef**
- 1 **cup salsa**
- 1 **can (4 ounces) chopped green chilies**
- 1 **envelope taco seasoning**
- 8 **frozen waffles**
  Shredded cheddar cheese, shredded lettuce, chopped tomatoes, cubed avocado, salsa and sour cream, optional

1. In a large skillet, cook beef over medium heat until no longer pink; drain. Stir in salsa, chilies and taco seasoning. Bring to a boil. Reduce heat; simmer for 5 minutes.

2. Meanwhile, toast waffles according to package directions. Serve with beef mixture and toppings of your choice.

Fun Fish Pastries

Kids and grown-ups alike will be positively hooked on these crab-stuffed pastries with their tantalizingly fishy shape. If you like, let your sandwich "swim" a bit in the cheese sauce.
—**MARY BALKAVICH** TYRONE, PA

PREP: 1 HOUR • **BAKE:** 15 MIN.
MAKES: 8 SERVINGS (2½ CUPS SAUCE)

- 1 **can (6 ounces) lump crabmeat, drained or light tuna in water**
- 1 **egg yolk**
- ⅛ **teaspoon each onion powder, garlic powder and salt**
- 2 **tablespoons shredded cheddar cheese**

PASTRY
- 3 **cups all-purpose flour**
- 1 **teaspoon salt**
- 1 **cup shortening**
- ⅓ **cup tomato juice**
- 1 **teaspoon Worcestershire sauce**

ASSEMBLY
- 1 **egg white, beaten**
- 1 **slice part-skim mozzarella cheese**
- 1 **pitted ripe olive, chopped**
  Curly endive and fresh blueberries, optional

SAUCE
- 1 **can (10¾ ounces) condensed cream of celery soup or cream of mushroom soup, undiluted**
- 1 **cup (4 ounces) shredded cheddar cheese**
- ¾ **cup 2% milk**
- 1 **jar (2 ounces) diced pimientos, drained**

1. In a small bowl, combine the crab, egg yolk, onion powder, garlic powder and salt. Stir in cheese; set aside.

2. For pastry, in a large bowl, combine flour and salt. Cut in shortening until mixture resembles coarse crumbs. Combine the tomato juice and Worcestershire sauce; stir into dry ingredients just until moistened. Turn onto a lightly floured surface and knead 8-10 times.

Family Quilt Pizza

Quilt pizzas are a blast to create. My family and friends get involved, and they come up with the most clever toppings and designs. Every slice looks different!

—MARIE LOUISE LUDWIG PHOENIXVILLE, PA

PREP: 30 MIN. • **BAKE:** 20 MIN.
MAKES: 6 SERVINGS

- 1 tube (13.8 ounces) refrigerated pizza crust
- 1 can (8 ounces) pizza sauce
- 4 cups (16 ounces) shredded part-skim mozzarella cheese
- 2 ounces sliced deli ham, cut into ½-in. strips
  Optional toppings: slices of sweet peppers, tomatoes, fully cooked sausage, mushrooms, ripe olives, pineapple, pepperoni, yellow summer squash and red onion; broccoli florets; crumbled feta cheese; and minced fresh basil and chives

1. Preheat oven to 425°. Unroll pizza crust and press to fit into a greased 15x10x1-in. baking pan, pinching edges to form a rim. Bake 8-10 minutes or until edges are lightly browned.
2. Spread crust with pizza sauce; top with mozzarella cheese. Using ham strips, outline 12 quilt sections. Arrange toppings of your choice in each section to create a patchwork design. Bake 10-15 minutes or until crust is golden brown and cheese is melted.

DID YOU KNOW?

Feta is a white, salty, semi-firm cheese. Although this type of cheese is mostly associated with Greek cuisine, the word "feta" comes from the Italian word *fette*, meaning "slice of food."

Cheesy Mac & Cheese

Cheesy Mac & Cheese

Everyone runs home for dinner when I announce that this homemade macaroni and cheese is on the menu. It also receives a lot of compliments at potlucks.

—DEBRA SULT CHANDLER, AZ

PREP: 20 MIN. • **BAKE:** 30 MIN.
MAKES: 8 SERVINGS

- 2 cups uncooked elbow macaroni
- 1 tablespoon all-purpose flour
- 1 cup heavy whipping cream
- 1 cup half-and-half cream
- ¼ cup sour cream
- 1 egg
- ½ teaspoon ground mustard
- ½ teaspoon cayenne pepper
- ¼ teaspoon salt
- ¼ teaspoon pepper
- ⅛ teaspoon ground nutmeg
- 8 ounces Monterey Jack cheese, cubed
- 8 ounces cheddar cheese, cubed
- 2 cups (8 ounces) shredded cheddar cheese

1. Cook macaroni according to package directions. Meanwhile, in a large bowl, whisk the flour, cream, half-and-half, sour cream, egg, mustard, cayenne, salt, pepper and nutmeg until smooth.
2. Drain pasta. Transfer to a greased 2½-qt. baking dish. Stir in cubed cheeses. Top with cream mixture. Sprinkle with shredded cheese.
3. Bake, uncovered, at 350° for 30-40 minutes or until bubbly and golden brown.

Family Quilt Pizza

Cheeseburger Cups

Cheeseburger Cups

A terrific recipe for moms with young kids and busy lives, this simple, inexpensive dish is table-ready in a half hour. Best of all, kids will go crazy for these darling dinner bites!

—JERI MILLHOUSE ASHLAND, OH

START TO FINISH: 30 MIN.
MAKES: 5 SERVINGS

- 1 pound ground beef
- ½ cup ketchup
- 2 tablespoons brown sugar
- 1 tablespoon prepared mustard
- 1½ teaspoons Worcestershire sauce
- 1 tube (12 ounces) refrigerated buttermilk biscuits
- ½ cup cubed process cheese (Velveeta)

1. In a large skillet, cook beef over medium heat until no longer pink; drain. Stir in ketchup, brown sugar, mustard and Worcestershire sauce. Remove from the heat; set aside.

2. Press each biscuit onto the bottom and up the sides of a greased muffin cup. Spoon beef mixture into cups; top with cheese cubes. Bake at 400° for 14-16 minutes or until golden brown.
FREEZE OPTION *Freeze cooled pastries in a freezer container, separating layers with waxed paper. To use, thaw pastries in the refrigerator for 8 hours. Reheat on a baking sheet in a preheated 375° oven until heated through.*

Grilled Cheese & Pepperoni

I wanted to add a little zip to my usual grilled cheese, so I used garlic bread spread instead of butter and added slices of pepperoni.

—JENNIFER ZUNIGA DENVER, CO

START TO FINISH: 20 MIN.
MAKES: 4 SANDWICHES

- 4 slices provolone cheese
- 4 slices cheddar cheese
- 16 slices pepperoni
- 12 red onion rings
- 8 slices Italian bread (½ inch thick)
- 4 teaspoons garlic spread

1. Layer the cheeses, pepperoni and onion on four bread slices; top with remaining bread. Spread outsides of sandwiches with garlic spread.
2. In a large skillet, toast sandwiches over medium heat for 2-4 minutes on each side or until golden brown and cheese is melted.

Corn Dog Twists

Kids will have as much fun making these twists on hot dogs and buns as they will eating them. Set out bowls of relish, mustard and ketchup for dunking.

—MELISSA TATUM GREENSBORO, NC

START TO FINISH: 25 MIN.
MAKES: 8 SERVINGS

- 1 tube (11½ ounces) refrigerated corn bread twists
- 8 hot dogs
- 1 tablespoon butter, melted
- 1 tablespoon grated Parmesan cheese

1. Separate corn bread twists; wrap one strip around each hot dog. Brush with butter; sprinkle with cheese. Place on a lightly greased baking sheet.
2. Bake at 375° for 11-13 minutes or until golden brown.

Corn Dog Twists

Bacon Cheeseburger Meatball Subs

I took two of my favorite foods, meatballs and bacon cheeseburgers, and rolled them into one delicious sandwich.

—CYNDY GERKEN NAPLES, FL

PREP: 40 MIN. • **BAKE:** 20 MIN.
MAKES: 8 SANDWICHES

- 2 eggs, lightly beaten
- 1 tablespoon Worcestershire sauce
- 2 medium onions, finely chopped
- ⅔ cup seasoned bread crumbs
- ⅓ cup grated Parmesan cheese
- 3 tablespoons minced fresh parsley or 1 tablespoon dried parsley flakes
- 8 garlic cloves, minced
- 2 tablespoons minced fresh basil or 2 teaspoons dried basil
- 1 tablespoon minced fresh oregano or 1 teaspoon dried oregano
- ⅛ teaspoon kosher salt
- ⅛ teaspoon pepper
- ⅛ teaspoon crushed red pepper flakes
- ¾ pound ground beef
- ⅔ pound ground veal
- ⅔ pound ground pork
- 24 cubes cheddar cheese (½-inch each)
- 8 cooked bacon strips, cut into thirds
- 8 lettuce leaves
- 8 submarine buns, split and toasted
- 1 cup barbecue sauce, warmed

1. In a large bowl, combine the first 12 ingredients. Crumble the ground meats over the mixture and mix well; divide into 24 portions.

2. Wrap each cheese cube with a cut bacon strip. Shape one portion of meat mixture around each bacon-wrapped cheese cube. Place meatballs on a greased rack in a shallow baking pan.

3. Bake, uncovered, at 400° for 20-25 minutes or until a thermometer reads 160°. Drain on paper towels. Serve meatballs on lettuce-lined buns with barbecue sauce.

Bacon Cheeseburger Meatball Subs

Mexican Chicken Penne for Kids

This hearty pasta dinner is packed with chicken, cheese and salsa flavor. Kids will devour it; adults will love it, too.

—MARTI GUTWEIN RENSSELAER, IN

START TO FINISH: 25 MIN.
MAKES: 6 SERVINGS

- 1 package (16 ounces) uncooked penne pasta
- 2 cups cubed cooked chicken
- 1¼ cups salsa con queso dip
- ½ cup milk
- ¼ teaspoon salt

1. Cook the pasta according to package directions. Meanwhile, in a large bowl, combine chicken, dip, milk and salt.
2. Drain pasta; return to pan. Stir in chicken mixture and toss to coat. Heat through.

ABC Melt

On the go? No problem! You can have this tangy sandwich ready for the road (or the table) in just 10 minutes.

—BARBARA NOWAKOWSKI

NORTH TONAWANDA, NY

START TO FINISH: 10 MIN.
MAKES: 2 SERVINGS

- 2 English muffins, split and toasted
- 2 teaspoons prepared mustard
- 4 slices Canadian bacon
- 1 medium apple, thinly sliced
- 4 slices Swiss cheese

Place muffin halves, cut side up, on an ungreased baking sheet. Spread with mustard; layer with Canadian bacon, apple slices and cheese. Bake at 350° for 5-6 minutes or until cheese is melted.

DID YOU KNOW?

Canadian bacon is actually closer to ham than bacon, despite a name that suggests otherwise. The Canadian bacon usually comes from a loin cut, making it leaner, but also more meaty, than regular bacon.

Popcorn & Pretzel Chicken Tenders

Popcorn & Pretzel Chicken Tenders

My daughter, Alivia, thought it would be tasty to coat chicken tenders with two of our favorite movie-watching snacks: popcorn and pretzels. Crunchy and crispy, this chicken and its creamy, sweet mustard sauce will delight you.

—SUZANNE CLARK PHOENIX, AZ

PREP: 25 MIN. + MARINATING
BAKE: 20 MIN.
MAKES: 6 SERVINGS (1 CUP SAUCE)

- 1½ pounds chicken tenderloins
- 1 cup buttermilk
- 2 teaspoons garlic powder
- 1 teaspoon salt
- 1 teaspoon onion powder
- ½ teaspoon pepper
- ¾ cup fat-free plain Greek yogurt
- ¼ cup peach preserves
- 1 tablespoon prepared mustard
- 4 cups miniature pretzels, crushed
- 2 cups air-popped popcorn, crushed
  Cooking spray

1. In a large bowl, combine the first six ingredients; toss to coat. Refrigerate, covered, at least 30 minutes. In a small bowl, mix yogurt, preserves and mustard; refrigerate until serving.
2. Preheat oven to 400°. In a large shallow dish, combine crushed pretzels and popcorn. Remove chicken from marinade, discarding marinade. Dip both sides of chicken in pretzel mixture, patting to help coating adhere. Place on a parchment paper-lined baking sheet; spritz with cooking spray.
3. Bake 20-25 minutes or until coating is golden brown and chicken is no longer pink. Serve with sauce.

Family-Friendly Stuffed Cheeseburgers

We were experimenting one night and came up with these tasty cheese-filled burgers. They're so good that we often don't even add condiments.

—**ALETHEA OSBORNE** FLORENCE, KY

PREP: 30 MIN. • **GRILL:** 10 MIN.
MAKES: 6 SERVINGS

- 1 **cup chopped sweet onion**
- ½ **cup crushed saltines (about 15 crackers)**
- 1 **egg**
- 1 **jalapeno pepper, seeded and minced**
- 1 **envelope ranch salad dressing mix**
- 1 **tablespoon Worcestershire sauce**
- 1 **garlic clove, minced**
- 1 **teaspoon pepper**
- 2 **pounds ground beef**
- 1½ **cups (6 ounces) shredded cheddar cheese**
- 1 **jar (4½ ounces) sliced mushrooms, drained**
- 3 **tablespoons cream cheese, softened**
- 6 **kaiser rolls, split**

1. In a large bowl, combine the first eight ingredients. Crumble beef over mixture and mix well. Shape into twelve thin patties.

2. Combine the cheddar cheese, mushrooms and cream cheese; spoon onto centers of six patties. Top with remaining patties; press edges firmly to seal.

3. Grill the burgers, covered, over medium heat or broil 4 in. from heat for 5-7 minutes on each side or until a thermometer reads 160° and juices run clear. Serve on rolls.

Chip-Crusted Chicken

Dijon-mayo and barbecue potato chips might sound strange together, but they make a delicious coating for chicken.

—**MIKE TCHOU** PEPPER PIKE, OH

START TO FINISH: 30 MIN.
MAKES: 6 SERVINGS

- ⅔ **cup Dijon-mayonnaise blend**
- 6 **cups barbecue potato chips, finely crushed**
- 6 **boneless skinless chicken breast halves (5 ounces each)**

1. Place mayonnaise blend and potato chips in separate shallow bowls. Dip chicken in mayonnaise blend, then coat with chips.

2. Place on an ungreased baking sheet. Bake at 375° for 20-25 minutes or until a thermometer reads 170°.

BBQ Meat Loaf Minis

Spice up the mini loaves by adding a cup of salsa and 2 teaspoons chili powder.

—**LINDA CALL** FALUN, KS

START TO FINISH: 30 MIN.
MAKES: 6 SERVINGS

- 1 **package (6 ounces) stuffing mix**
- 1 **cup water**
- 2 **tablespoons hickory smoke-flavored barbecue sauce**
- 1 **pound ground beef**
- 1 **cup (4 ounces) shredded cheddar cheese**
  Additional hickory smoke-flavored barbecue sauce, optional

1. Preheat oven to 375°. In a large bowl, combine stuffing mix, water and 2 tablespoons barbecue sauce. Add beef; mix lightly but thoroughly. Place ⅓ cup mixture into each of 12 ungreased muffin cups, pressing lightly.

2. Bake, uncovered, 18-22 minutes or until a thermometer reads 160°. Sprinkle tops with cheese; bake 2-4 minutes longer or until cheese is melted. If desired, serve with additional barbecue sauce.

FREEZE OPTION *Securely wrap and freeze cooled meat loaves in plastic wrap and foil. To use, partially thaw in refrigerator overnight. Unwrap meat loaves; reheat on a greased shallow baking pan in a preheated 350° oven until heated through and a thermometer inserted in center reads 165°.*

BBQ Meat Loaf Minis

Three-Cheese Ham Loaf

½   pound Italian turkey sausage
links, casings removed
½   cup chopped sweet onion
4   cans (8 ounces each)
no-salt-added tomato sauce
3   ounces sliced turkey pepperoni
1   tablespoon sugar
½   teaspoon dried parsley flakes
½   teaspoon dried basil
9   ounces uncooked whole wheat
spaghetti
3   tablespoons grated Parmesan
cheese
12   fresh mozzarella cheese pearls
12   slices pimiento-stuffed olives

1. In a large nonstick skillet, cook the beef, sausage and onion over medium heat 6-8 minutes or until meat is no longer pink, breaking up meat into crumbles; drain.

2. Stir in tomato sauce, pepperoni, sugar, parsley and basil. Bring to a boil. Reduce heat; simmer, uncovered, 20-25 minutes or until thickened. Meanwhile, cook spaghetti according to package directions.

3. Drain spaghetti; toss with sauce. Sprinkle with Parmesan cheese. Top each serving with two cheese pearls and two olive slices to resemble eyes.

FREEZE OPTION *Do not cook or add spaghetti. Freeze cooled beef mixture in freezer containers. To use, partially thaw in refrigerator overnight. Cook spaghetti according to package directions. Place beef mixture in a large skillet; heat through, stirring occasionally and adding a little water if necessary. Proceed as directed.*

Three-Cheese Ham Loaf

Convenient refrigerated dough is the base for this golden loaf stuffed with ham and cheese.
—GLORIA LINDELL WELCOME, MN

PREP: 15 MIN. • **BAKE:** 30 MIN.
MAKES: 6 SERVINGS

1   tube (13.8 ounces) refrigerated
pizza crust
10   slices deli ham
¼   cup sliced green onions
1   cup (4 ounces) shredded
part-skim mozzarella cheese
1   cup (4 ounces) shredded cheddar
cheese
4   slices provolone cheese
1   tablespoon butter, melted

1. Unroll the dough onto a greased baking sheet; top with the ham, onions and cheeses. Roll up tightly jelly-roll style, starting with a long side; pinch seam to seal and tuck ends under. Brush with butter.

2. Bake at 350° for 30-35 minutes or until golden brown. Let stand for 5 minutes; cut into 1-in. slices.
FREEZE OPTION *Cool unsliced loaf on a wire rack. Spray a large piece of foil with cooking spray. Wrap loaf in prepared foil and freeze for up to 3 months. To use, thaw at room temperature for 2 hours. Preheat oven to 350°. Unwrap and place on a greased baking sheet. Bake 15-20 minutes or until heated through. Let stand 5 minutes; cut into 1-in. slices.*

Supernatural Spaghetti

I got the idea for my pizza-flavored spaghetti when I saw someone dip a slice of pizza into a pasta dish. My wife and kids love it, and so do my friends.
—ROBERT SMITH LAS VEGAS, NV

PREP: 20 MIN. • **COOK:** 30 MIN.
MAKES: 6 SERVINGS

½   pound lean ground beef
(90% lean)

Supernatural Spaghetti

Chicken Nugget Casserole

1 tube (12 ounces) refrigerated buttermilk biscuits

1. Preheat the oven to 350°. In a large bowl, combine soup, turkey, mushrooms, peas, milk and the seasonings. Pour into a greased 8-in.-square baking dish; arrange biscuits over top.
2. Bake, uncovered, 20-25 minutes or until biscuits are golden brown.

Pizza Macaroni & Cheese

My grandma made this for us once during a visit, and I never forgot just how good it was. Since my kids love anything with pepperoni and cheese, I bake it so they can enjoy it as much as I did.
—JULI MEYERS HINESVILLE, GA

PREP: 30 MIN. • **BAKE:** 25 MIN.
MAKES: 12 SERVINGS

- **2 packages (14 ounces each) deluxe macaroni and cheese dinner mix**
- **½ cup sour cream**
- **1 can (14½ ounces) petite diced tomatoes, drained**
- **1 can (15 ounces) pizza sauce**
- **1 small green pepper, chopped**
- **1 small sweet red pepper, chopped**
- **2 cups (8 ounces) shredded Italian cheese blend**
- **2 ounces sliced pepperoni**

1. Preheat oven to 350°. Cook macaroni according to package directions for al dente. Drain; return to pan. Stir in contents of cheese packets and sour cream. Transfer to a greased 13x9-in. baking dish.
2. In a small bowl, combine the tomatoes and pizza sauce; drop by spoonfuls over macaroni. Top with the peppers, cheese and pepperoni. Bake, uncovered, 25-30 minutes or until bubbly.

TOP TIP

To make sure pasta is done, use a fork to remove a single piece of pasta from the boiling water. Rinse the pasta in cold water and taste. Pasta should be cooked until al dente, or firm yet tender.

Chicken Nugget Casserole

Our kids love to eat chicken nuggets this way. Add spaghetti and a salad on the side for a satisfying supper.
—TYLENE LOAR MESA, AZ

PREP: 5 MIN. • **BAKE:** 30 MIN.
MAKES: 4-6 SERVINGS

- **1 package (13½ ounces) frozen chicken nuggets**
- **⅓ cup grated Parmesan cheese**
- **1 can (26½ ounces) spaghetti sauce**
- **1 cup (4 ounces) shredded part-skim mozzarella cheese**
- **1 teaspoon Italian seasoning**

1. Place chicken nuggets in a greased 11x7-in. baking dish. Sprinkle with Parmesan cheese. Layer with the spaghetti sauce, mozzarella cheese and Italian seasoning.
2. Cover and bake at 350° for 30-35 minutes or until chicken is heated through and cheese is melted.

Biscuit Turkey Bake

Although I'm in college, I still get a kick out of opening a tube of refrigerated biscuits. My friends go crazy for this casserole.
—STEPHANIE DENNING MOUNT PLEASANT, IA

START TO FINISH: 30 MIN.
MAKES: 5 SERVINGS

- **1 can (10¾ ounces) condensed cream of chicken soup, undiluted**
- **1 cup chopped cooked turkey or chicken**
- **1 can (4 ounces) mushroom stems and pieces, drained**
- **½ cup frozen peas**
- **¼ cup 2% milk**
- **Dash each ground cumin, dried basil and thyme**

Round Out Your Meals

Whether you need a soup, bread, side dish or salad to complete your lunch or dinner, you'll find the perfect recipe to gobble up here!

Easy Slow Cooker Mac & Cheese

Easy Slow Cooker Mac & Cheese

My sons always tell me, "You're the best mom in the world!" whenever I make this creamy mac and cheese perfection. Does it get any better than that?
—HEIDI FLEEK HAMBURG, PA

PREP: 25 MIN. • **COOK:** 1 HOUR
MAKES: 8 SERVINGS

- 2 cups uncooked elbow macaroni
- 1 can (10¾ ounces) condensed cheddar cheese soup, undiluted
- 1 cup 2% milk
- ½ cup sour cream
- ¼ cup butter, cubed
- ½ teaspoon onion powder
- ¼ teaspoon white pepper
- ⅛ teaspoon salt
- 1 cup (4 ounces) shredded cheddar cheese
- 1 cup (4 ounces) shredded fontina cheese
- 1 cup (4 ounces) shredded provolone cheese

1. Cook macaroni according to package directions for al dente. Meanwhile, in a large saucepan, combine soup, milk, sour cream, butter and seasonings; cook and stir over medium-low heat until blended. Stir in cheeses until melted.
2. Drain macaroni; transfer to a greased 3-qt. slow cooker. Stir in the cheese mixture. Cook, covered, on low 1-2 hours or until heated through.

Kids' Favorite Chili

Warm the whole family up on a cold night with a heaping pot of chili. The recipe has been in my family for three generations.
—TERRI KEENEY GREELEY, CO

START TO FINISH: 25 MIN.
MAKES: 4 SERVINGS

- 1 pound ground turkey
- ½ cup chopped onion
- 1 can (15¾ ounces) pork and beans
- 1 can (14½ ounces) diced tomatoes, undrained
- 1 can (10¾ ounces) condensed tomato soup, undiluted
- 1 tablespoon brown sugar
- 1 tablespoon chili powder

In a large saucepan, cook turkey and onion over medium heat until meat is no longer pink; drain. Stir in the remaining ingredients. Bring to a boil. Reduce heat; cover and simmer for 15-20 minutes or until heated through.

Cheese Fries

I came up with this recipe after my daughter had cheese fries at a restaurant and couldn't stop talking about them.
—MELISSA TATUM GREENSBORO, NC

Cheese Fries

START TO FINISH: 20 MIN.
MAKES: 8-10 SERVINGS

- 1 package (28 ounces) frozen steak fries
- 1 can (10¾ ounces) condensed cheddar cheese soup, undiluted
- ¼ cup 2% milk
- ½ teaspoon garlic powder
- ¼ teaspoon onion powder
  Paprika

1. Arrange the steak fries in a single layer in two greased 15x10x1-in. baking pans. Bake at 450° for 15-18 minutes or until fries are tender and golden brown.
2. Meanwhile, in a saucepan, combine the soup, milk, garlic powder and onion powder; heat through. Drizzle over fries; sprinkle with paprika.

Turtle Bread

My son Nick and his friends would always ask me to bake this turtle-shaped bread. Nick's brother and sister would join in to help me mix and knead the dough. That's when the flour really started flying!

—ELIZABETH INGARGIOLA GALLOWAY, NJ

PREP: 30 MIN. + RISING
BAKE: 35 MIN. + COOLING
MAKES: 1 LOAF

- 2¼ to 2¾ cups all-purpose flour
- 1 tablespoon sugar
- 1 package (¼ ounce) quick-rise yeast
- 1 teaspoon salt
- ½ cup water
- ⅓ cup milk
- 1 tablespoon butter
- 2 eggs
- 2 raisins

1. In a large bowl, combine 2 cups flour, sugar, yeast and salt. In a small saucepan, heat the water, milk and butter to 120°-130°. Add to dry ingredients; beat just until moistened. Add 1 egg; beat until smooth. Stir in enough remaining flour to form a soft dough.

2. Turn onto a floured surface; knead until smooth and elastic, about 6-8 minutes. Cover and let rest for 10 minutes. Shape dough into one 2-in. ball, four 1½-in. balls, one 1-in. ball and one large round ball.

3. For turtle shell, place the large dough ball in the center of a greased baking sheet. Place the 2-in. ball at the top for head; position 1½-in. balls on either side for feet. Shape the 1-in. ball into a triangle for tail; place on opposite side of large ball from head.

4. Press all edges together to seal. Add raisins for eyes. Cover and let rise in a warm place until doubled, about 25 minutes.

5. Beat the remaining egg; brush over dough. With a sharp knife, make shallow diamond-shaped slashes across top of turtle shell.

6. Bake at 350° for 35-40 minutes or until golden brown. Remove to a wire rack to cool.

Turtle Bread

Green Flop Jell-O

Green Flop Jell-O

Get ready for fluffy lemon-lime goodness that kids of all ages will love. Better yet, you can adjust this recipe and try it with any flavor Jell-O.

—**MICHELLE GAUER** SPICER, MN

PREP: 15 MIN. + CHILLING
MAKES: 16 SERVINGS (¾ CUP EACH)

- 2 **cups lemon-lime soda**
- 2 **packages (3 ounces each) lime gelatin**
- 6 **ounces cream cheese, softened**
- 2 **cups lemon-lime soda, chilled**
- 1 **carton (12 ounces) frozen whipped topping, thawed**

1. Microwave 2 cups soda on high for 1-2 minutes or until hot. Place hot soda and gelatin in a blender; cover and process until gelatin is dissolved. Add cream cheese; process until blended.
2. Transfer to a large bowl; stir in the chilled soda. Whisk in whipped topping. Pour into a 3-qt. trifle bowl or glass bowl. Refrigerate, covered, 4 hours or until firm.

Watermelon Convertible Fruit Salad

What could be cooler than a convertible in the summer? You'll have as much fun as we did when you make this whimsical watermelon treat.

—*TASTE OF HOME* TEST KITCHEN

PREP: 1 HOUR
MAKES: 6-8 SERVINGS

- 1 **miniature seedless watermelon (about 3 pounds)**
- 1 **fresh strawberry, halved**
- 5 **lime slices**
- 1 **seedless red grape**
- 1 **large marshmallow, cut in half**
- 1 **can (11 ounces) mandarin oranges, drained**
- 1 **cup green grapes**

1. With a long sharp knife, cut a thin slice from watermelon so melon lies flat. Using a small sharp knife, lightly score a horizontal cutting line around middle of the melon, leaving 3 in. on each side of stem end unscored for the windshield. Next, score a vertical line over top of melon, connecting both ends of the horizontal line.

2. Using the long knife, cut through melon along the vertical cutting line. (Stop cutting at the horizontal cutting line.) Then, cut through melon along the horizontal cutting line. Gently pull away top portion of car.
3. Cut a thin slice from the end of the top portion for the convertible top. Trim slice to fit on tail end of car; set aside. Remove fruit from both portions of melon; cut into balls or cubes and set aside. Attach convertible top with toothpicks.
4. For side mirrors, cut a 1¼-in. notch from each lower corner of windshield. Place a strawberry half in each notch; attach with toothpicks. For windshield, using a sharp razor blade or small knife, score a ¾-in. frame around perimeter of windshield.

Carefully remove watermelon rind within frame of windshield.
5. For wheels, attach two lime slices with toothpicks to each side of melon. Cut the remaining lime slice in half. Using a toothpick, place one lime portion centered below windshield for a mouth.
6. For eyebrows, remove fruit from the remaining half slice; cut peel into two pieces. For eyes, cut ends from red grape and cut grape crosswise in half. Using toothpicks, add grape halves to the marshmallow halves and position on windshield; attach eyebrows. If desired, add a mandarin orange smile.
7. In a large bowl, combine the green grapes and remaining mandarin oranges with reserved watermelon. Spoon into car.

Watermelon Convertible Fruit Salad

Loaded Waffle Fries

Fried Mashed Potato Balls

The key to making this recipe is to use mashed potatoes that are firm from chilling. Serve the potato balls with sour cream or ranch salad dressing on the side.
—**TASTE OF HOME** TEST KITCHEN

PREP: 25 MIN. + STANDING
COOK: 5 MIN./BATCH
MAKES: 6 SERVINGS

- 2 cups cold mashed potatoes
- 1 egg, lightly beaten
- ¾ cup shredded cheddar cheese
- ½ cup chopped green onions
- ¼ cup real bacon bits
- ½ cup dry bread crumbs
  Oil for frying

1. Place mashed potatoes in a large bowl; let stand at room temperature for 30 minutes. Stir in the egg, cheese, onions and bacon bits. Shape into 1-in. balls; roll in bread crumbs. Let stand for 15 minutes.
2. In an electric skillet, heat 1 in. of oil to 375°. Fry potato balls, a few at a time, for 2½ to 3 minutes or until golden brown. Remove with a slotted spoon to paper towels to drain. Serve warm.

Fried Mashed Potato Balls

Loaded Waffle Fries

Make any meal better with these special fries. I top them with a savory blend of cheese, scallions and bacon. A family favorite paired with hot dogs or burgers, they're super fun as a snack, too.
—**JEFFREY VICCONE** DECATUR, IL

START TO FINISH: 30 MIN.
MAKES: 4 SERVINGS

- 4 cups frozen waffle-cut fries
- ½ to 1½ teaspoons steak seasoning
- 1 cup (4 ounces) shredded cheddar cheese
- 2 tablespoons chopped green onions
- 2 tablespoons real bacon bits

1. Arrange waffle fries in a greased 15x10x1-in. baking pan. Bake at 450° for 20-25 minutes or until lightly browned.
2. Sprinkle with steak seasoning; toss to combine. Top with remaining ingredients. Bake 2-3 minutes longer or until cheese is melted.
NOTE *This recipe was tested with McCormick's Montreal Steak Seasoning. Look for it in the spice aisle.*

Banana Split Fruit Salad

Whether you're celebrating or just relaxing after a long day, you'll definitely enjoy these charming parfaits. Watermelon, bananas and raspberries combine for a deliciously healthy treat.
—**TASTE OF HOME** TEST KITCHEN

START TO FINISH: 20 MIN.
MAKES: 4 SERVINGS

- 2 medium bananas
- ¼ medium seedless watermelon
- 1 carton (6 ounces) vanilla custard-style yogurt
- 1 cup fresh raspberries
- ¼ cup chopped walnuts

1. Cut each banana in half widthwise. Cut each half into four pieces lengthwise. Using an ice cream scoop, scoop four balls from watermelon (save remaining melon for another use).
2. Arrange four banana pieces in each of four shallow dessert bowls; top with watermelon. Spoon yogurt over melon. Sprinkle with raspberries and walnuts. Serve immediately.

Pepperoni Pizza Soup

until smooth. Pour into apple juice mixture. Stir in yogurt and, if desired, food coloring. Cover and refrigerate for at least 2 hours or until chilled.

3. Ladle soup into bowls. Combine sour cream and milk; spoon about 2½ teaspoons into the center of each bowl. Using a toothpick, pull mixture out, forming a flower or design of your choice.

Movie Theater Pretzel Rods

My kids and all of their friends clamor for these large, chewy pretzel rods, which are fantastic fresh from the oven.

—LISA SHAW BURNETTSVILLE, IN

PREP: 70 MIN. + RISING • **BAKE:** 10 MIN.
MAKES: 32 PRETZEL RODS

- 1 package (¼ ounce) active dry yeast
- 1½ cups warm water (110° to 115°)
- 2 tablespoons sugar
- 2 tablespoons butter, melted
- 1½ teaspoons salt
- 4 to 4½ cups all-purpose flour
- 8 cups water
- ½ cup baking soda
- 1 egg yolk
- 1 tablespoon cold water
  Coarse salt, optional

1. In a large bowl, dissolve yeast in warm water. Add the sugar, butter, salt and 2 cups flour. Beat until smooth. Stir in enough remaining flour to form a soft dough (dough will be sticky).

2. Turn dough onto a floured surface; knead until smooth and elastic, about 6-8 minutes. Place in a greased bowl, turning once to grease top. Cover and let rise in a warm place until doubled, about 1 hour.

3. In a large saucepan, bring 8 cups water and baking soda to a boil. Punch dough down; divide into 32 portions. Roll each into a 5-in. log. Add to boiling water, a few at a time, for 30 seconds. Remove with a slotted spoon; drain on paper towels. Place on greased baking sheets. Lightly beat the egg yolk and cold water; brush over pretzels. Sprinkle with coarse salt if desired. Bake at 425° for 9-11 minutes or until golden brown. Remove from pans to wire racks. Serve warm.

Pepperoni Pizza Soup

My husband and I used to own a pizzeria, and this dish was always popular on the menu. I still make the soup for all kinds of potlucks and gatherings, and people constantly ask for the recipe.

—ESTELLA PETERSON MADRAS, OR

PREP: 20 MIN. • **COOK:** 8¼ HOURS
MAKES: 6 SERVINGS (2¼ QUARTS)

- 2 cans (14½ ounces each) Italian stewed tomatoes, undrained
- 2 cans (14½ ounces each) reduced-sodium beef broth
- 1 small onion, chopped
- 1 small green pepper, chopped
- ½ cup sliced fresh mushrooms
- ½ cup sliced pepperoni, halved
- 1½ teaspoons dried oregano
- ⅛ teaspoon pepper
- 1 package (9 ounces) refrigerated cheese ravioli
  Shredded part-skim mozzarella cheese and sliced ripe olives

1. In a 4-qt. slow cooker, combine the first eight ingredients. Cook, covered, on low 8-9 hours.

2. Stir in ravioli; cook, covered, on low 15-30 minutes or until pasta is tender. Top servings with cheese and olives.

Strawberry Soup

When I first prepared this change-of-pace soup for a party, it was a hit. My husband always likes it warmed up, but I prefer it chilled, so it's a good thing it tastes fabulous either way! We drizzle leftovers on top of frozen custard for a fresh, fruity topping.

—SHARON DELANEY-CHRONIS
SOUTH MILWAUKEE, WI

PREP: 20 MIN. + CHILLING
MAKES: 7 SERVINGS

- 1 cup water, divided
- 1 cup unsweetened apple juice
- ⅔ cup sugar
- ½ teaspoon ground cinnamon
- ⅛ teaspoon ground cloves
- 2 cups fresh strawberries, hulled
- 2 cups strawberry yogurt
- 2 to 3 drops red food coloring, optional
- ¼ cup sour cream
- 2 tablespoons milk

1. In a large saucepan, combine ¾ cup water, apple juice, sugar, cinnamon and cloves. Bring to a boil, stirring occasionally. Remove from the heat.

2. Place strawberries and remaining water in a blender; cover and process

ABC Soup

Instead of opening a store-bought can of alphabet soup, why not make some from scratch? Kids of all ages love this traditional soup with a tomato base, ground beef and alphabet pasta.

—**SHARON BROCKMAN** APPLETON, WI

START TO FINISH: 30 MIN.
MAKES: 11 SERVINGS (2¾ QUARTS)

- 1 **pound ground beef**
- 1 **medium onion, chopped**
- 2 **quarts tomato juice**
- 1 **can (15 ounces) mixed vegetables, undrained**
- 1 **cup water**
- 2 **beef bouillon cubes**
- 1 **cup uncooked alphabet pasta**
  Salt and pepper to taste

In a large saucepan, cook beef and onion over medium heat until the meat is no longer pink; drain. Add tomato juice, vegetables, water and bouillon; bring to a boil. Add pasta. Cook, uncovered, for 6-8 minutes or until pasta is tender, stirring frequently. Add salt and pepper.

NOTE *If you don't have small pasta on hand for ABC Soup, use quick-cooking barley or instant rice. Cook until tender. If you're out of bouillon cubes, 2 teaspoons of bouillon granules can be used instead.*

Cauliflower Popcorn

Roasting cauliflower transforms it into a delectable snack. Your family will eat it up just like popcorn. It's up to you whether you reveal it's actually a vegetable!

—*TASTE OF HOME* TEST KITCHEN

START TO FINISH: 30 MIN.
MAKES: 4 SERVINGS

- 1 **large head cauliflower, broken into small florets**
- 1 **tablespoon olive oil**
- ½ **teaspoon garlic salt**
- 1 **tablespoon grated Parmesan cheese**

Place the cauliflower in a greased 15x10x1-in. baking pan. Drizzle with oil and sprinkle with garlic salt; toss to coat. Bake, uncovered, at 400° for 15-18 minutes or until tender, stirring once. Sprinkle with cheese.

ABC Soup

Bacon Cheeseburger Buns

Here's a fun way to serve bacon cheeseburgers to a group without all the fuss of assembling sandwiches at the last minute. Offer ketchup or barbecue sauce on the side for dipping.

—MARJORIE MILLER HAVEN, KS

PREP: 1 HOUR + RISING • **BAKE:** 10 MIN.
MAKES: 2 DOZEN

- 2 **packages (¼ ounce each) active dry yeast**
- ⅔ **cup warm water (110° to 115°)**
- ⅔ **cup warm milk (110° to 115°)**
- ¼ **cup sugar**
- ¼ **cup shortening**
- 2 **eggs**
- 2 **teaspoons salt**
- 4½ to 5 **cups all-purpose flour**

FILLING
- 1 **pound sliced bacon, diced**
- 2 **pounds ground beef**
- 1 **small onion, chopped**
- 1½ **teaspoons salt**
- ½ **teaspoon pepper**
- 1 **pound process cheese (Velveeta), cubed**
- 3 to 4 **tablespoons butter, melted**
  Ketchup or barbecue sauce, optional

1. In a large bowl, dissolve yeast in warm water. Add the milk, sugar, shortening, eggs, salt and 3½ cups flour; beat until smooth. Stir in enough remaining flour to form a soft dough.
2. Turn onto a floured surface; knead until smooth and elastic, about 6-8 minutes. Place in a greased bowl, turning once to grease top. Cover and let rise in a warm place until doubled, about 1 hour.
3. Meanwhile, in a large skillet, cook bacon over medium heat until crisp. Using a slotted spoon, remove to paper towels. In a Dutch oven, cook the beef, onion, salt and pepper over medium heat until meat is no longer pink; drain. Add bacon and cheese; cook and stir until cheese is melted. Remove from the heat.
4. Punch dough down. Turn onto a lightly floured surface; divide into fourths. Roll each portion into an 12x8-in. rectangle; cut each into six squares. Place ¼ cup meat mixture in the center of each square. Bring corners together in the center and pinch to seal.
5. Place 2 in. apart on greased baking sheets. Bake at 400° for 9-11 minutes or until lightly browned. Brush with butter. Serve warm, with ketchup or barbecue sauce if desired.

Chilled Blueberry Soup

With 100 blueberry bushes in my garden, I'm always looking for recipes calling for this sweet-tart fruit. I was delighted when my granddaughter shared this one with me.

—EDITH RICHARDSON JASPER, AL

PREP: 5 MIN. • **COOK:** 10 MIN. + CHILLING
MAKES: 4 SERVINGS

- ½ **cup sugar**
- 2 **tablespoons cornstarch**
- 2¾ **cups water**
- 2 **cups fresh or frozen blueberries**
- 1 **cinnamon stick (3 inches)**
- 1 **can (6 ounces) frozen orange juice concentrate**
  Sour cream, optional

1. In a large saucepan, combine sugar and cornstarch. Gradually stir in water until smooth. Bring to a boil over medium heat; cook and stir for 2 minutes or until thickened.
2. Add blueberries and cinnamon stick; return to a boil. Remove from the heat. Stir in the orange juice concentrate until thawed. Cover and refrigerate for at least 1 hour. Discard cinnamon stick. Garnish with sour cream if desired.

Chilled Blueberry Soup

Nacho Hash Brown Casserole

Nacho Hash Brown Casserole

Toss cubed potatoes into the slow cooker with the right ingredients and you'll get the best hash browns ever! This cheesy side will complement most main dishes.

—**PAT HABIGER** SPEARVILLE, KS

PREP: 15 MIN. • **COOK:** 3¼ HOURS
MAKES: 8 SERVINGS

- 1 package (32 ounces) frozen cubed hash brown potatoes, thawed
- 1 can (10¾ ounces) condensed cream of celery soup, undiluted
- 1 can (10¾ ounces) condensed nacho cheese soup, undiluted
- 1 large onion, finely chopped
- ⅓ cup butter, melted
- 1 cup (8 ounces) reduced-fat sour cream

In a greased 3-qt. slow cooker, combine the first five ingredients. Cover and cook on low for 3-4 hours or until potatoes are tender. Stir in sour cream. Cover and cook 15-30 minutes longer or until heated through.

Peanut Butter & Jelly Bites

My friend is an avid runner. After I heard that she craved a peanut butter and jelly sandwich during a race, I whipped up these convenient bites for her.

—**JENNIFER HEASLEY** YORK, PA

PREP: 25 MIN. • **BAKE:** 15 MIN. + COOLING
MAKES: 2 DOZEN

- 4 ounces cream cheese, softened
- ½ cup strawberry jelly, divided
- 2 tubes (8 ounces each) refrigerated seamless crescent dough sheets
- ½ cup creamy peanut butter
- 1 cup confectioners' sugar
- 5 tablespoons 2% milk

1. Preheat oven to 350°. In a small bowl, beat the cream cheese and ¼ cup jelly until smooth. Unroll each sheet of crescent dough into a rectangle. Spread each with half of the filling to within ½ in. of edges. Roll up jelly-roll style, starting with a long side; pinch seam to seal. Cut each roll widthwise into 12 slices; place on parchment paper-lined baking sheets, cut side down.

2. Bake 12-15 minutes or until golden brown. Cool rolls on pans 2 minutes. Remove to wire racks to cool.

3. In a small bowl, beat peanut butter, confectioners' sugar and milk until smooth. Drizzle over rolls; top with remaining jelly.

Bunny Pear Salad

All dressed up, these darling bunny salads make an adorable side dish for your next family feast.

—**ALBERTINE SPERLING** ABBOTSFORD, BC

START TO FINISH: 15 MIN.
MAKES: 4 SERVINGS

Red lettuce leaves
- 1 can (15¼ ounces) pear halves, drained
- 12 dried currants or raisins
- 8 whole almonds
- 4 baby carrots
- 4 parsley sprigs
Whipped cream in a can

1. Arrange lettuce on four salad plates; place a pear half cut side down on each plate. For eyes, insert two currants at narrow end of pear; add one currant for nose. For ears, insert almonds upright behind eyes.

2. With a sharp knife, cut a small hole at one end of each carrot; insert a parsley sprig for carrot top. Place under bunny's nose. For tail, spray a small mound of whipped cream at the wide end of each pear.

Bunny Pear Salad

**Dutch Apple
Pie Muffins**

mixture by tablespoonfuls into the center of each muffin. Sprinkle with topping.

4. Bake at 400° for 20-24 minutes or until a toothpick inserted in muffin comes out clean. Cool for 5 minutes before removing from pan to a wire rack. Combine glaze ingredients; drizzle over muffins. Serve warm.

Biscuit Bowl Chili

Kids love to help make these biscuit bowls almost as much as they like eating them. For another weeknight option, fill the cups with taco-flavored or sloppy joe meat.

—**CASSY RAY** PARKERSBURG, WV

PREP: 20 MIN. • **COOK:** 30 MIN.
MAKES: 8 SERVINGS

- 1 **tube (16.3 ounces) large refrigerated flaky biscuits**
- 2 **teaspoons cornmeal**
- 1 **pound lean ground beef (90% lean)**
- ½ **cup chopped onion**
- 1 **can (16 ounces) kidney beans, rinsed and drained**
- 1 **can (11½ ounces) V8 juice**
- 1 **cup ketchup**
- 2 **teaspoons chili powder**
- ½ **teaspoon salt**
- ¼ to ½ **teaspoon cayenne pepper**
- ¼ **teaspoon crushed red pepper flakes**
- ¼ **teaspoon pepper**
- ½ **cup shredded cheddar cheese**

1. Preheat oven to 350°. Place two muffin tins upside down; spray bottoms and sides of eight alternating muffin cups. On a work surface, roll or press biscuits into 4-in. circles. Sprinkle both sides with cornmeal, pressing lightly to adhere. Place biscuits over greased muffin cups, shaping biscuits around cups.

2. Bake 11-13 minutes or until lightly browned. Carefully remove biscuit bowls from pans; cool on a wire rack.

3. Meanwhile, in a large skillet, cook beef and onion over medium heat 6-8 minutes or until beef is no longer pink; drain. Stir in beans, V8 juice, ketchup and seasonings. Bring to a boil. Reduce heat; simmer, covered, 10 minutes. Serve in biscuit bowls; top with cheese.

Dutch Apple Pie Muffins

Delight loved ones with a fresh batch of these cinnamon-spiced muffins. The crumbly, streusel-like topping makes them a treat, too.

—**SUZANNE PAULEY** RENTON, WA

PREP: 25 MIN. • **BAKE:** 20 MIN.
MAKES: 1 DOZEN

- 2 **cups finely chopped peeled tart apples**
- 3 **tablespoons sugar**
- 3 **tablespoons water**
- 2 **tablespoons brown sugar**
- 1 **tablespoon all-purpose flour**
- 2 **tablespoons butter**
- 1 **teaspoon lemon juice**
- 1 **teaspoon vanilla extract**

TOPPING
- 3 **tablespoons brown sugar**
- 2 **tablespoons all-purpose flour**
- 2 **tablespoons quick-cooking oats**
- 2 **tablespoons cold butter**

BATTER
- 1¾ **cups all-purpose flour**
- ½ **cup sugar**
- 2 **teaspoons baking powder**

- 1 **teaspoon ground cinnamon**
- ½ **teaspoon salt**
- 1 **egg**
- ¾ **cup 2% milk**
- ¼ **cup canola oil**

GLAZE
- ¼ **cup confectioners' sugar**
- 1 **to 2 teaspoons 2% milk**

1. In a small saucepan, combine the apples, sugar, water and brown sugar. Bring to a boil over medium heat. Sprinkle with flour; cook and stir for 2 minutes or until thickened. Stir in butter and lemon juice. Remove from the heat; add vanilla. Set aside to cool.

2. For topping, combine the brown sugar, flour and oats. Cut in butter until mixture resembles coarse crumbs; set aside.

3. In a large bowl, combine the flour, sugar, baking powder, cinnamon and salt. In another bowl, beat the egg, milk and oil. Stir into the dry ingredients just until moistened. Fill greased or paper-lined muffin cups three-fourths full. Drop apple

Chicken Alphabet Soup

Watermelon Shark

Chicken Alphabet Soup

I'm a teenager and I love to make this chicken soup for my family. It makes me so happy when they tell me how much they like it.

—**SARAH MACKEY** NEW SMYRNA BEACH, FL

START TO FINISH: 25 MIN.
MAKES: 10 SERVINGS (2½ QUARTS)

- 3 **medium carrots, chopped**
- 2 **celery ribs, chopped**
- ¾ **cup chopped sweet onion**
- 1 **tablespoon olive oil**
- 2 **quarts chicken broth**
- 3 **cups cubed cooked chicken breast**
- ¼ **teaspoon dried thyme**
- 1½ **cups uncooked alphabet pasta**
- 3 **tablespoons minced fresh parsley**

In a Dutch oven, saute the carrots, celery and onion in oil until tender. Stir in the broth, chicken and thyme. Bring to a boil. Stir in alphabet pasta. Reduce heat; simmer, uncovered, for 10 minutes or until pasta is tender. Stir in parsley.

Watermelon Shark

Take a bite out of boredom with this kid-friendly food project. Little ones will let out a scream of joy when they see it!

—*TASTE OF HOME* **TEST KITCHEN**

PREP: 1 HOUR
MAKES: 32 SERVINGS

- 1 **large watermelon**
- 2 **cups seedless red grapes**
- 1 **medium cantaloupe, peeled, seeded and cubed**
- 2 **cups fresh blueberries**
- 2 **medium oranges**
- 1 **jar (12 ounces) pineapple preserves**
  Swedish Fish candies, optional

1. Using a large sharp knife, cut off one end of the watermelon so that watermelon stands at an angle. Using a razor blade or small knife, score an opening for the mouth. With knife, cut out and remove mouth. Cut out triangles for teeth; remove rind from teeth.

2. For shark fin, cut a triangle from removed rind; attach to shark with toothpicks. For eyes, attach two grapes with toothpicks.

3. Remove the fruit from inside the watermelon; cut into cubes. In a large bowl, combine watermelon, cantaloupe, blueberries and remaining grapes. Finely grate peel from oranges and squeeze juice. In a small bowl, mix preserves, orange juice and peel; add to fruit and toss gently.

4. Stand shark on a platter. Fill the opening with some of the fruit mixture; add a few Swedish Fish if desired. Serve with remaining fruit.

TOP TIP

For the very best blueberries, pick ones that are firm, plump and smooth-skinned. In addition, the color is important. Good blueberries should be deep purple-blue to blue-black; reddish ones aren't yet ripe.

Candy Bar Apple Salad

This creamy, sweet salad with a crisp apple crunch is a real people-pleaser. The recipe yields a lot, which is good, because it tends to go fast.

—CYNDI FYNAARDT OSKALOOSA, IA

START TO FINISH: 15 MIN.
MAKES: 12 SERVINGS (¾ CUP EACH)

- 1½ cups cold 2% milk
- 1 package (3.4 ounces) instant vanilla pudding mix
- 1 carton (8 ounces) frozen whipped topping, thawed
- 4 large apples, chopped (about 6 cups)
- 4 Snickers candy bars (1.86 ounces each), cut into ½-inch pieces

In a large bowl, whisk the milk and pudding mix for 2 minutes. Let stand for 2 minutes or until soft-set. Fold in whipped topping. Fold in apples and candy bars. Refrigerate until serving.

Hot Dog Potato Soup

If you prefer, you can use leftover meatballs instead of hot dogs and leftover corn in place of frozen in this chowder-like soup. You can also use any cheese blend you have on hand.

—JEANNIE KLUGH LANCASTER, PA

START TO FINISH: 15 MIN.
MAKES: 5 SERVINGS

- 2 cans (18.8 ounces each) ready-to-serve chunky baked potato with cheddar and bacon bits soup
- 4 hot dogs, halved lengthwise and sliced
- 1 cup (4 ounces) shredded cheddar-Monterey Jack cheese
- 1 cup frozen corn
- 1 cup milk

In a large microwave-safe bowl, combine all the ingredients. Cover and microwave on high for 8-10 minutes or until heated through, stirring every 2 minutes.
NOTE *This recipe was tested in a 1,100-watt microwave.*

Candy Bar Apple Salad

Special Seasonal Treats

Take a journey through an entire year's worth of delicious eats and sweets. The menu is all set for your next big gathering or party!

Winter Wonderland Cereal Treats

Round up your little helpers—they can lend a hand here by decorating with gumdrops, pretzels and candies. Airheads Sour Belts make sweet scarves; snipped marshmallows work for hats.

—BRENDA AUSTIN MANLIUS, NY

START TO FINISH: 30 MIN.
MAKES: ABOUT 10 TREES OR 6 SNOWMEN

- ¼ cup butter, cubed
- 2 teaspoons ground cinnamon or pumpkin pie spice
- 1 package (10 ounces) large marshmallows
- 6 cups Rice Krispies
  Pretzel sticks, assorted candies and/or Fruit Roll-Ups, cut into thin strips
  Vanilla frosting
  Flaked coconut

1. In a large saucepan, melt butter over medium heat. Add cinnamon and marshmallows; stir until blended and the marshmallows are melted. Remove from the heat. Stir in cereal until coated. Use mixture to shape trees or snowmen.

2. For trees, press mixture into a greased 13x9-in. baking pan; cool completely. Cut into triangles.
3. For snowmen, cool cereal mixture slightly; shape into different-sized balls using buttered hands. Stack balls to make snowmen.
4. To decorate, attach pretzels, candies and/or Fruit Roll-Ups with frosting. Arrange cereal treats on a platter; surround with coconut. Serve the same day for best texture.

Gingerbread Ice Cream Sandwiches

When it comes to making an ice cream sandwich, not all gingerbread men are created equal: Some are too crisp, while others are too soft. These thin yet sturdy boys hold up nicely in the freezer and make for a playful make-ahead dessert.

—*TASTE OF HOME* TEST KITCHEN

PREP: 30 MIN. + CHILLING
BAKE: 10 MIN./BATCH + FREEZING
MAKES: 1 DOZEN

- 3 cups vanilla ice cream
- ¾ teaspoon ground cinnamon

COOKIES
- ⅓ cup butter, softened

Gingerbread Ice Cream Sandwiches

- ½ cup packed brown sugar
- 1 egg
- ⅓ cup molasses
- 2 cups all-purpose flour
- 1 teaspoon ground ginger
- ¾ teaspoon baking soda
- ¾ teaspoon ground cinnamon
- ½ teaspoon ground cloves
- ¼ teaspoon salt

1. In a blender, combine ice cream and cinnamon. Transfer to a freezer container; freeze for at least 2 hours.
2. Meanwhile, in a large bowl, cream the butter and brown sugar until light and fluffy. Add egg, then molasses. Combine flour, ginger, baking soda, cinnamon, cloves and salt; gradually add to creamed mixture and mix well. Cover and refrigerate 2 hours or until easy to handle.
3. Preheat oven to 350°. On a lightly floured surface, roll dough to ⅛-in. thickness. Cut with a floured 3½-in. gingerbread-shaped cookie cutter. Place 1 in. apart on ungreased baking sheets. Bake 8-10 minutes or until the edges are firm. Remove to wire racks to cool.
4. To make ice cream sandwiches, spread ¼ cup softened ice cream over the bottom of half of the cookies; top with remaining cookies. Wrap each in plastic wrap; freeze on a baking sheet at least 1 hour.

Winter Wonderland Cereal Treats

Elf Cookies

A sweet frosting glaze, colorful candies and well-placed almond slices turn these sugar cookie diamonds into a big batch of Santa's helpers. Bake a batch of the adorable elves as a classroom treat or use a few to brighten up each of your cookie trays.

—*TASTE OF HOME* TEST KITCHEN

PREP: 45 MIN. • **BAKE:** 10 MIN.
MAKES: 28 COOKIES

- ½ **tube refrigerated sugar cookie dough, softened**
- ⅓ **cup all-purpose flour**
- 2½ **cups confectioners' sugar**
- 10 **teaspoons water**
- 4 **teaspoons meringue powder**
  Assorted food coloring
  Assorted sprinkles, candies and almond slices

1. Preheat oven to 350°. In a small bowl, beat cookie dough and flour until combined. Roll out on a lightly floured surface to ⅛-in. thickness. Cut with a floured 1¾x3¼-in. diamond cookie cutter. Place 2 in. apart on ungreased baking sheets. Bake 7-9 minutes or until edges are golden brown. Remove to wire racks to cool.

2. In a large bowl, combine the confectioners' sugar, water and meringue powder; beat on low speed just until blended. Beat on high 4-5 minutes or until stiff peaks form. Divide icing into portions and tint as desired. Keep unused icing covered at all times with a damp cloth. If necessary, beat again on high speed to restore texture.

3. Frost and decorate cookies as desired with assorted sprinkles and candies; add almonds for ears.

TOP TIP

If you're struggling with cookie dough sticking to your cutter, try placing a piece of plastic wrap loosely over the dough. When you press down the cookie cutter, the plastic wrap will keep it dough-free.
—**GAYLE B.** MILLBROOK, AL

Elf Cookies

Snowflake
Tomato Soup

Pretzel Wreaths

Snowflake Tomato Soup

This sensational soup packs lots of pleasing ingredients, and it's a delight to eat when decorated with a pretty snowflake. It'll warm you up right up on a chilly day.

—*TASTE OF HOME* TEST KITCHEN

START TO FINISH: 25 MIN.
MAKES: 8-10 SERVINGS

- 2 **cans (28 ounces each) crushed tomatoes**
- 1 **can (14½ ounces) chicken broth**
- 2 **tablespoons minced fresh oregano or 2 teaspoons dried oregano**
- 1 **to 2 tablespoons sugar**
- 1 **cup heavy whipping cream**
- ⅓ **cup sour cream**

1. In a blender, process tomatoes, one can at a time, until smooth. Transfer to a large saucepan. Stir in the broth; bring to a boil. Reduce heat; cover and simmer for 10 minutes. Stir in the oregano and sugar. Add a small amount of hot tomato mixture to whipping cream; return all to the saucepan. Cook until slightly thickened (do not boil).

2. Cut a small hole in the corner of a pastry or plastic bag; fill with sour cream. Pipe a snowflake on each bowl of soup.

Pretzel Wreaths

Our two girls help me measure, pour, stir, shape and, of course, eat these chewy pretzel rounds when they're done! If you can manage to spare a batch (good luck with that!), they make adorable Christmas gifts.

—**ROBERTA SPIEKER** FORT COLLINS, CO

PREP: 45 MIN. • **BAKE:** 15 MIN.
MAKES: 16 PRETZELS

- 1 **package (¼ ounces) active dry yeast**
- 1½ **cups warm water (110° to 115°)**
- 4 **cups all-purpose flour**
- 1 **tablespoon sugar**
- 1 **teaspoon salt**
- 1 **egg white, lightly beaten**
  Coarse salt or colored sugar

1. In a large bowl, dissolve yeast in water. Add 2 cups flour, sugar and salt. Beat until smooth. Stir in enough remaining flour to form a soft dough.

2. Turn onto a floured surface; knead the dough until smooth and elastic, about 6 minutes. Cover and let rest for 15 minutes. Preheat the oven to 425°.

3. Divide dough into 16 portions. Roll each portion into a 15-in. rope. Fold each rope in half and twist two or three times; shape into a circle and pinch ends together.

4. Place on greased baking sheets. Brush with the egg white; sprinkle with the salt or sugar. Bake for 12-15 minutes.

Jolly Ginger Reindeer Cookies

I made gingerbread cookies for years before realizing my gingerbread-man cutter becomes a reindeer when turned upside down. They're super crispy and festive!

—SUE GRONHOLZ BEAVER DAM, WI

PREP: 50 MIN. + CHILLING
BAKE: 10 MIN./BATCH + COOLING
MAKES: ABOUT 4 DOZEN

- ½ cup butter, softened
- 1 cup packed brown sugar
- 1 egg
- ¾ cup molasses
- 3½ cups all-purpose flour
- 2 teaspoons ground ginger
- 1 teaspoon baking powder
- 1 teaspoon baking soda
- 1 teaspoon ground cinnamon
- 1 teaspoon ground allspice

ROYAL ICING
- 2 cups confectioners' sugar
- 2 tablespoons plus 2 teaspoons water
- 4 teaspoons meringue powder
- ¼ teaspoon cream of tartar
- 1 to 2 tablespoons miniature semisweet chocolate chips
- 1 to 2 tablespoons Red Hots

1. In a large bowl, cream butter and brown sugar until light and fluffy. Beat in egg and molasses. In another bowl, whisk flour, ginger, baking powder, baking soda, cinnamon and allspice; gradually beat into creamed mixture.
2. Divide dough in half. Shape each into a disk; wrap in plastic wrap. Refrigerate 1 hour or until firm enough to roll.
3. Preheat oven to 350°. On a lightly floured surface, roll each portion of dough to ¼-in. thickness. Cut with a floured 3-in. gingerbread boy-shaped cookie cutter. Place 1 in. apart on greased baking sheets.
4. Bake 10-12 minutes or until set. Cool on pans 1 minute. Remove to wire racks to cool completely.
5. In a bowl, combine confectioners' sugar, water, meringue powder and cream of tartar; beat on low speed just until blended. Beat on high 4-5 minutes or until stiff peaks form. Keep unused icing covered at all times with a damp cloth. If necessary, beat again on high speed to restore texture.
6. To decorate the cookies, place gingerbread boys on a work surface with heads facing you. Pipe antlers onto legs. With icing, attach chocolate chips for eyes and Red Hots for noses. Let stand until set. Store in airtight containers.

Layered Christmas Gelatin

My jewel-toned gelatin always makes an appearance during our Christmas feast. Filled with cranberries and pineapple, the sweet-tart salad could even serve as a light dessert.

—DIANE SCHEFELKER IRETON, IA

PREP: 30 MIN. + CHILLING
MAKES: 10 SERVINGS

- 1 package (3 ounces) lime gelatin
- 1 cup boiling water
- ⅓ cup unsweetened pineapple juice
- 1 cup crushed pineapple, drained

CREAM CHEESE LAYER
- 1 teaspoon unflavored gelatin
- 2 tablespoons cold water
- 1 package (8 ounces) cream cheese, softened
- ⅓ cup milk

BERRY LAYER
- 2 packages (3 ounces each) strawberry gelatin
- 2 cups boiling water
- 1 can (14 ounces) whole-berry cranberry sauce
  Whipped topping, optional

1. Dissolve lime gelatin in boiling water; stir in pineapple juice. Stir in pineapple. Pour into an 11x7-in. dish; refrigerate until set.
2. In a small saucepan, sprinkle unflavored gelatin over cold water; let stand for 1 minute. Heat over low heat, stirring until gelatin is completely dissolved. Transfer to a small bowl. Beat in cream cheese and milk until smooth. Spread over lime layer; refrigerate until set.
3. Dissolve strawberry gelatin in boiling water; stir in cranberry sauce. Cool for 10 minutes. Carefully spoon over cream cheese layer. Refrigerate until set.
4. Cut into squares. Garnish with whipped topping if desired.

Jolly Ginger Reindeer Cookies

Good Green Fun

ST. PADDY'S RAINBOW

Tip your hat to St. Pat with a rainbow of assorted crisp multicolored munchies. Toss in some cauliflower clouds for a whimsical touch. Suddenly, even the littlest leprechauns will be happy to gobble up their veggies. What luck!

Reuben Appetizers

Each year, I round up appetizer recipes for an annual party we throw for friends and family. These tidbits are always a big hit.

—PAT BOHN OREGON CITY, OR

START TO FINISH: 15 MIN.
MAKES: 4 DOZEN

- ½ cup Thousand Island salad dressing
- 4 plain bagels, split
- 2 to 3 large dill pickles, sliced lengthwise
- 1 pound thinly sliced deli corned beef
- 8 slices Swiss cheese

1. Spread salad dressing on each bagel half. Top with pickle slices, corned beef and cheese. Place on an ungreased baking sheet.
2. Broil 6 in. from the heat for 4-6 minutes or until the cheese is melted. Cut each into six wedges; serve immediately.

Lime Milk Shakes

My daughter likes to make these delicious shakes in our blender. I sometimes turn them into freezer pops, and often switch up their flavors for different occasions by using orange or rainbow sherbet and orange juice concentrate.

—CRYSTAL SHECKLES-GIBSON
BEESPRING, KY

START TO FINISH: 10 MIN.
MAKES: 6 SERVINGS

- 2¼ cups milk
- ¾ cup thawed limeade concentrate
- 3 cups lime sherbet, softened

Place all ingredients in a blender; cover and process until smooth. Pour into chilled glasses; serve immediately.

Lime Milk Shakes

COLOR CUES

The Rainbow Cake at left is both easy and impressive. Simply pipe the rings in this order: red, orange, yellow, green, blue and purple. The photo above shows the cake before a final layer of white batter is piped over the purple ring, creating the bottom arch of the rainbow.

Rainbow Cake with Clouds

Rainbow Cake with Clouds

This spectacular dessert stands on its own—no frosting needed! For decorating, use a little whipped cream to make fluffy clouds, and you're done. Your guests will think this cake is as good as finding a pot of gold!

—JANET TIGCHELAAR JERSEYVILLE, ON

PREP: 30 MIN. • **BAKE:** 40 MIN. + COOLING
MAKES: 16 SERVINGS

- 1 **package white cake mix (regular size)**
  Purple, blue, green, yellow, orange and red paste food coloring
- 1 **cup heavy whipping cream**
- 3 **tablespoons confectioners' sugar**
- ½ **teaspoon vanilla extract**

1. Preheat oven to 325°. Grease and flour a 10-in. fluted tube pan. Prepare the cake mix according to package directions. Transfer 1⅓ cups batter to prepared pan; spread evenly. Remove an additional 2 tablespoons batter to a small bowl; reserve.

2. Divide the remaining batter into six separate bowls, tinting each with food coloring to make the following: 2 tablespoons purple batter, ¼ cup blue batter, ⅓ cup green batter, ½ cup yellow batter, ⅔ cup orange batter, and the remaining batter red.

3. Fill six small food-safe plastic bags with a different color batter. Cut a small hole in a corner of the red batter bag; pipe a wide ring onto white batter to within ½ in. of pan edges. Pipe a ring of orange in the middle of the red ring,

leaving some red visible on each side. Repeat by piping remaining colors in the middle of the previous layer, in rainbow color order. (Each ring will be narrower than the previous layer.) Fill a bag with reserved white batter; pipe over purple ring only.

4. Bake 40-45 minutes or until a toothpick inserted in center comes out clean. Cool completely in pan on a wire rack.

5. Remove cake from pan; place on a serving plate. In a bowl, beat cream until it begins to thicken. Add confectioners' sugar and vanilla; beat until soft peaks form. Serve cake with whipped cream clouds.

NOTE *To remove cakes easily, use solid shortening to grease plain and fluted tube pans.*

Hop, Hop, Hooray!

BUNNY PANCAKES

Kick off Easter with this cute creation. Start with a pancake mix so you can hightail it out of the kitchen in minutes. Don't forget to shape a few flapjacks for ears and feet.

On individual plates, stack the pancakes as seen in the photo. Make a tail with a dollop of whipped cream and shredded coconut. Banana slices and mini chocolate chips become sweet little details for the bunny feet.

Easter Bunny Treats

Easter Bunny Treats

Our whole family had a blast making these bunny-riffic marshmallow stacks together. The result is beyond cute!

—HOLLY JOST MANITOWOC, WI

START TO FINISH: 15 MIN.
MAKES: 1 DOZEN

- ⅔ **cup vanilla frosting**
- 30 **large marshmallows**
  Pink gel or paste food coloring
  Red and pink heart-shaped decorating sprinkles
- 60 **miniature marshmallows**

1. Frost the tops of 12 large marshmallows; stack a large marshmallow on top of each. Quarter the remaining large marshmallows; set aside for ears. Tint ¼ cup frosting pink. Cut a small hole in the corner of a pastry or plastic bag; place pink frosting in bag.

2. Pipe a ribbon between the stacked marshmallows for bow tie. With white frosting, attach red hearts for eyes and a pink heart for nose. Pipe pink whiskers and smile.

3. For ears, pipe the center of quartered marshmallows pink; attach to head with white frosting. With the remaining white frosting, attach the miniature marshmallows for legs and tail. Let stand until dry.

Chicks-on-the-Ranch Deviled Eggs

A hint of Dijon mustard, Parmesan cheese and ranch salad dressing take the flavor of these absolutely adorable deviled eggs to new heights.

—TASTE OF HOME TEST KITCHEN

START TO FINISH: 25 MIN.
MAKES: ½ DOZEN

- 6 hard-cooked eggs
- ¼ cup shredded Parmesan cheese
- ¼ cup prepared ranch salad dressing
- 1 teaspoon Dijon mustard
  Dash pepper
- 5 carrot chips
- 12 capers
  Fresh dill sprigs

1. Cut a thin slice from the bottom of each egg so it sits flat. Cut the top third from each egg. Carefully remove yolks and place in a small bowl; mash with a fork. Add the cheese, salad dressing, mustard and pepper; stir until well blended. Spoon into the egg white bottoms; replace tops.

2. Cut 12 feet and 12 small triangles for beaks from carrot chips. Gently press capers into the filling for eyes; add beaks. Insert a dill sprig in top of each egg for tuft of feathers. Place feet in front of chicks. Chill until serving.

Bacon Breakfast Cups

Chicks-on-the-Ranch Deviled Eggs

Bacon Breakfast Cups

My son joked about adding bacon to cupcakes, then I made these bacon cups the next morning. The look on his face was priceless!

—KAREN BURKETT RESEDA, CA

PREP: 30 MIN. • **BROIL:** 5 MIN.
MAKES: 6 SERVINGS

- 18 turkey bacon strips, cut in half
- 1 cup frozen shredded hash brown potatoes
- 2 eggs
- 2 teaspoons 2% milk
  Dash each salt and pepper
- 2 teaspoons butter
- ¼ cup shredded Mexican cheese blend
  Chopped green onion and fresh parsley

1. Preheat the oven to 375°. Line 12 alternating cups in a mini-muffin pan with bacon pieces, crisscrossing three strips in each so they resemble spokes of a wheel. Loosely crumple twelve 3-in. strips of aluminum foil into balls; place in cups to keep bacon from sliding. Bake 15-20 minutes or until bacon is crisp.

2. Meanwhile, cook the potatoes according to package directions. In a small bowl, whisk eggs, milk, salt and pepper. In a small skillet, heat butter over medium heat. Pour in the egg mixture; cook and stir until eggs are thickened and no liquid egg remains.

3. Transfer bacon cups to a baking sheet; remove foil. Spoon hash browns and scrambled eggs into cups; sprinkle with cheese. Broil 3-4 in. from heat 3-5 minutes or until cheese is melted. Sprinkle with green onion and parsley.

Red, White & Blue Sips

JULY 4TH LAYERED DRINKS

All you need for these colorful beverages are cranberry-apple juice, white pina colada drink and blue low-cal Gatorade. The secret is in the sugar—the heaviest sugar content goes on the bottom. Start with the cranberry juice, then fill the glass with ice. Next slowly pour in the pina colada drink and the G2 Gatorade, making sure to pour each new beverage directly onto ice. With a little bit of patience and lots of ice, you can create a star-spangled hit.

—KATRINA BAHL

INKATRINASKITCHEN.COM

Fudgy Patriotic Brownies

I always come home with an empty pan when I take these to potlucks or parties.

—JULIE MOYER UNION GROVE, WI

PREP: 25 MIN. • **BAKE:** 35 MIN. + COOLING
MAKES: 2 DOZEN

- 1 **cup butter, cubed**
- 4 **ounces unsweetened chocolate, chopped**
- 2 **cups sugar**
- 1 **teaspoon vanilla extract**
- 4 **eggs**
- 1¼ **cups all-purpose flour**
- ½ **teaspoon salt**
- 1 **cup chopped pecans**

FROSTING

- ¼ **cup butter, cubed**
- 2 **ounces unsweetened chocolate, chopped**
- 3 **cups confectioners' sugar**
- 5 **to 6 tablespoons milk**
- 1 **teaspoon vanilla extract**
  Red, white and blue decorating icing

1. In a microwave-safe bowl, melt butter and chocolate; stir until smooth. Stir in sugar and vanilla. Add eggs, one at a time, stirring well after each addition. Combine the flour and salt; stir into chocolate mixture until combined. Stir in pecans.

2. Spread into a greased 13x9-in. baking dish. Bake at 325° for 35-40 minutes or until a toothpick inserted near the center comes out clean. Cool on a wire rack.

3. For frosting, in a small heavy saucepan, melt butter and chocolate over low heat; stir until smooth. Remove from the heat. Stir in the confectioners' sugar, milk and vanilla until blended.

4. Frost brownies; score into 24 bars. Using a small star-shaped cookie cutter, lightly press a star outline in the center of each brownie. Outline stars with red, white and blue icing.

Fudgy Patriotic Brownies

**Uncle Sam's
Crispy Treat Cake**

Patriotic Gelatin Salad

Almost as spectacular as the fireworks, this lovely salad makes quite a "bang" at patriotic celebrations. It's exciting to serve, and friends and family love the cool fruity and creamy layers.

—**SUE GRONHOLZ** BEAVER DAM, WI

PREP: 20 MIN. + CHILLING
MAKES: 16 SERVINGS

    2 **packages (3 ounces each)
       berry blue gelatin**
    2 **packages (3 ounces each)
       strawberry gelatin**
    4 **cups boiling water, divided**
2½ **cups cold water, divided**
    2 **envelopes unflavored gelatin**
    2 **cups milk**
    1 **cup sugar**
    2 **cups (16 ounces) sour cream**
    2 **teaspoons vanilla extract**

1. In four separate bowls, dissolve each package of gelatin in 1 cup boiling water. Add ½ cup cold water to each and stir. Pour one bowl of blue gelatin into a 10-in. fluted tube pan coated with cooking spray; chill until almost set, about 30 minutes.
2. Set other three bowls of gelatin aside at room temperature. Soften unflavored gelatin in remaining cold water; let stand 5 minutes.
3. Heat the milk in a saucepan over medium heat just below boiling. Stir in softened gelatin and sugar until sugar is dissolved. Remove from heat; stir in sour cream and vanilla until smooth. When the blue gelatin in the pan in almost set, carefully spoon 1½ cups sour cream mixture over it. Chill until almost set, about 30 minutes.
4. Carefully spoon one bowl of strawberry gelatin over cream layer. Chill until almost set. Carefully spoon 1½ cups cream mixture over the strawberry layer. Chill until almost set. Repeat, adding layers of blue gelatin, cream mixture and strawberry gelatin, chilling in between each. Chill several hours or overnight.
NOTE *This recipe takes time to prepare since each layer must be set before the next layer is added.*

Uncle Sam's Crispy Treat Cake

Decorating the two-piece stovepipe hat may take awhile, but I think you'll find it easy and rewarding.

—**ANNIE RUNDLE** MUSKEGO, WI

PREP: 1¼ HOURS
MAKES: 24 SERVINGS

    8 **cups miniature marshmallows**
   ½ **cup butter, cubed**
  12 **cups crisp rice cereal**
2½ **cups shortening**
    3 **cups confectioners' sugar**
   ¾ **teaspoon vanilla extract**
    3 **jars (7 ounces each) marshmallow
       creme**
       Red and blue paste food coloring

1. In a Dutch oven, combine the marshmallows and cubed butter. Cook and stir over medium-low heat until melted. Remove from the heat; stir in cereal. Press 4 cups into a greased 9-in. round pan. Form remaining mixture into a 5-in.-diameter x 6½-in.-tall cylinder; place on waxed paper to cool.

2. For frosting, in a large bowl, beat shortening until fluffy; beat in confectioners' sugar and vanilla until smooth. Beat in marshmallow creme until light and fluffy.
3. Unmold cereal mixture from the 9-in. pan and place on a cake plate. Place 3 cups frosting in a small bowl; beat in red food coloring until smooth. Frost top and sides of 9-in. cake with 1 cup red frosting.
4. Place 1 cup white frosting in a small bowl; beat in blue food coloring until smooth. For hatband, frost bottom 2¼ in. of the cylinder with blue frosting. Place cylinder on cake. Frost the rest of cylinder with red frosting.
5. Cut a small hole in the corner of a pastry or plastic bag; insert #48 basketweave tip. Using white frosting, pipe stripes on sides of hat. With a #7 round tip, pipe trim on edges of hatband and around top edge of hat.
6. Using a 1½-in. star cookie cutter, press a row of stars onto hatband. Fill in stars with white frosting using the #7 tip.

Cream Cheese Cutouts

Decorating cookies always puts me in a happy mood. Cookies from this recipe don't rise a lot or lose their shape, making them perfect for decorating.
—JULIE DAWSON GALENA, OH

PREP: 15 MIN. + CHILLING
BAKE: 10 MIN./BATCH + COOLING
MAKES: ABOUT 7 DOZEN

- 1 cup butter, softened
- 1 package (3 ounces) cream cheese, softened
- 1 cup sugar
- ¼ teaspoon salt
- 1 egg
- 1 teaspoon vanilla extract
- 2½ cups all-purpose flour

FROSTING

- 3 cups confectioners' sugar
- ⅓ cup butter, softened
- 1½ teaspoons vanilla extract
- 2 to 3 tablespoons 2% milk

Food coloring, optional
Assorted sprinkles or candies

1. In a large bowl, cream butter, cream cheese, sugar and salt until light and fluffy. Beat in egg and vanilla. Gradually beat in flour. Refrigerate, covered, 1-2 hours or until firm enough to roll.

2. Preheat oven to 375°. On a lightly floured surface, roll dough to ⅛-in. thickness. Cut with floured cookie cutters. Place 1 in. apart on ungreased baking sheets.

3. Bake 7-8 minutes or until edges are lightly browned. Cool on pans 1 minute. Remove to wire racks to cool completely.

4. In a small bowl, beat confectioners' sugar, butter, vanilla and enough milk to reach desired consistency. If desired, add food coloring. Decorate cookies with frosting and sprinkles.

Mom's Tangerine Iced Tea

Mom's Tangerine Iced Tea

Take a sip of this sweet tea with a citrus twist. You'll love it.
—MARY MILLER POPLARVILLE, MS

PREP: 10 MIN. • **COOK:** 5 MIN. + CHILLING
MAKES: 4 SERVINGS

- 2¾ cups water, divided
- 4 individual black tea bags
- ⅔ cup sugar
- 2 cups fresh tangerine juice (about 12 tangerines)
  Ice cubes
  Tangerine slices and mint sprigs, optional

1. In a small saucepan, bring 2 cups water to a boil. Remove from the heat; add tea bags. Steep for 3-5 minutes. Discard tea bags; cool tea slightly.

2. In another saucepan, combine remaining water and sugar; bring to a boil. Cook and stir until sugar is dissolved. Remove from the heat; cool slightly.

3. Transfer tea and sugar syrup to a large pitcher; stir in tangerine juice. Refrigerate until chilled.

4. Serve over ice; add tangerine slices and mint if desired.

Cream Cheese Cutouts

Meat Lovers' Snack Mix

Everyone will go wild for this crunchy appetizer on game day. My husband especially loves that it features all of his favorite foods: meats, salted nuts and hot sauce.

—**GINA MYHILL-JONES** 100 MILE HOUSE, BC

PREP: 15 MIN. • **BAKE:** 50 MIN. + COOLING
MAKES: 6 CUPS

- 1¼ cups wasabi-coated green peas
- ¾ cup salted peanuts
- 3 pepperoni-flavored meat snack sticks (1½ ounces each), cut into bite-size pieces
- 2 ounces beef jerky, cut into bite-size pieces
- ½ cup corn nuts
- ½ cup Rice Chex
- ½ cup Multi Grain Cheerios
- ½ cup crunchy cheese puff snacks
- 2 tablespoons chopped sun-dried tomatoes (not packed in oil)
- ⅓ cup canola oil
- 1½ teaspoons chili powder
- 1½ teaspoons onion powder
- ½ teaspoon hot pepper sauce
- ½ teaspoon soy sauce
- ¼ teaspoon seasoned salt

1. Preheat oven to 250°. Combine first nine ingredients in a large bowl. In a small bowl, whisk oil, chili powder, onion powder, pepper sauce, soy sauce and seasoned salt. Drizzle over cereal mixture and toss to coat.

2. Spread into a greased 15x10x1-in. baking pan. Bake 50 minutes, stirring every 10 minutes. Cool completely on a wire rack. Store in an airtight container.

DID YOU KNOW?

Wasabi, a popular Japanese version of horseradish, has quite the kick of fiery-hot flavor. It's traditionally used as a condiment with sushi and sashimi, but many sauces, mustards and snack items are seasoned with wasabi now.

Meat Lovers'
Snack Mix

Candy Corn Quesadillas

Celebrate the season with a savory touch. These candy corn triangles will be a super smash hit. Let kids join in the fun by using a rolling pin to crush a bag filled with nacho tortilla chips while you do the rest.

—MARIE PARKER MILWAUKEE, WI

PREP: 25 MIN. • **COOK:** 10 MIN.
MAKES: 2 DOZEN

- 1 **rotisserie chicken, cut up**
- 1 **jar (16 ounces) salsa**
- 1 **cup frozen corn, thawed**
- ¼ **cup barbecue sauce**
- ½ **teaspoon ground cumin**
- ½ **cup butter, melted**
- 8 **flour tortillas (10 inches)**
- 1 **jar (15½ ounces) salsa con queso dip, warmed**
- 4 **cups (16 ounces) shredded Mexican cheese blend**
- 2⅔ **cups crushed nacho-flavored tortilla chips**
- ½ **cup sour cream**

1. In a Dutch oven, combine the first five ingredients; heat through, stirring occasionally. Brush butter over one side of each tortilla.

2. Place one tortilla in a large skillet, buttered side down. Spread with 1 cup chicken mixture; top with another tortilla, buttered side up. Cook over medium heat 1-2 minutes or until bottom is lightly browned. Turn quesadilla.

3. Spread ½ cup queso dip over quesadilla; carefully sprinkle cheese along outer edge. Cook, covered, 1-2 minutes or until cheese begins to melt.

4. Remove to a cutting board. Sprinkle crushed chips over queso dip. Cut quesadilla into six wedges. Place a small dollop of sour cream at the point of each wedge. Repeat with remaining ingredients.

TOP TIP

Have leftover tortillas? Create breakfast burritos by spooning scrambled eggs and salsa on them, or cover them with peanut butter, apple butter and cream cheese for quick on-the-go sandwiches.

Candy Corn Quesadillas

Pudding Poltergeists

Spooky Snacks

Pudding Poltergeists

Ghostly yet colorful, these enchanting treats take on big personality with a touch of candy on top. Little kids would love to make them disappear.
—*TASTE OF HOME* TEST KITCHEN

START TO FINISH: 25 MIN.
MAKES: 7 SERVINGS

- 1 package (2.7 ounces) French vanilla mousse mix
- 3 drops each neon blue, green and purple food coloring
  Assorted decorations: cake decorator hearts, red decorating gel, and purple and red Nerds

1. Prepare mousse mix according to package directions; divide into three portions. Tint one portion blue, one green and one purple.
2. Transfer each to a pastry or plastic bag; cut a hole in one corner of each bag. Pipe ghost shapes into 5-oz. plastic cups. Decorate just before serving.

Halloween Candy Bark

My kids and I wanted to make a dessert using the beautiful colors of fall and some leftover Halloween candy. Let your imagination go wild when selecting ingredients.
—**MARGARET BROTT**
COLORADO SPRINGS, CO

PREP: 20 MIN. + STANDING
MAKES: 2¾ POUNDS

- 2 teaspoons butter
- 1½ pounds white candy coating, coarsely chopped
- 2 cups pretzels, coarsely chopped
- 10 Oreo cookies, chopped
- ¾ cup candy corn
- ¾ cup dry roasted peanuts
- ½ cup milk chocolate M&M's
- ½ cup Reese's Pieces

1. Line a 15x10x1-in. baking pan with foil; grease foil with butter. In a microwave, melt candy coating; stir until smooth. Spread into prepared pan. Sprinkle with remaining ingredients; press into candy coating. Let stand about 1 hour.
2. Break or cut bark into pieces. Store in an airtight container.

Spooky Snacks

These clever crawlers are made in a snap, and it's an ideal recipe to let children do from start to finish.
—**ANDREA CHAPMAN** HELENA, OK

START TO FINISH: 15 MIN.
MAKES: 2 DOZEN

- ½ cup plus 1 tablespoon peanut butter
- 48 butter-flavored crackers
- ⅔ cup chow mein noodles
- ¼ cup raisins

Spread 1 teaspoon of peanut butter on the tops of 24 crackers. Place four noodles on each side of each cracker; top with the remaining crackers. Spread a small amount of peanut butter on each raisin; place two on each cracker for eyes.

Frankie Cupcakes

These cupcakes are sure to impress (and spook!) folks. Be prepare— the bites will disappear quickly!

—*TASTE OF HOME* **TEST KITCHEN**

PREP: 45 MIN. • **MAKES:** VARIED

Pretzel sticks
Large marshmallows
Corn syrup
Green colored sugar
1 **can (16 ounces) vanilla frosting**
Purple and black paste food coloring
Cupcakes of your choice
Purple nonpareils
Candy-coated licorice, spearmint leaves and Nerds candies
1 **can (16 ounces) chocolate frosting**

1. Insert a pretzel stick into a flat end of each marshmallow. Using a clean paint brush, lightly coat the marshmallows with corn syrup. Immediately roll top and sides in green colored sugar; allow to dry for 20 minutes.

2. Meanwhile, set aside ¼ cup vanilla frosting. Tint remaining vanilla frosting purple and spread over cupcakes. Roll edge of each cupcake in nonpareils; set aside.

3. To decorate face, press candy-coated licorice bolts into each side of marshmallow. Cut a small piece of spearmint leaf into an eyebrow, press cut side onto face. Using remaining vanilla frosting, pipe eyes; add Nerd candy eyeballs. Pipe chocolate frosting onto faces for mouths and stitches as desired.

4. Carefully insert pretzel stick into the center of each cupcake. Tint remaining chocolate frosting black. Using pastry tip #233, add black hair.

5. If desired, use black frosting to pipe the collar of a suit jacket outline. Fill in the center with black.

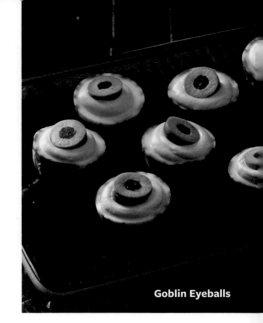

Goblin Eyeballs

Goblin Eyeballs

Guests at your Halloween party will be "goblin" up these edible eyeballs.

—*TASTE OF HOME* **TEST KITCHEN**

PREP: 40 MIN. + STANDING
MAKES: 2 DOZEN

12 **eggs**
Red food coloring
¾ **cup mayonnaise**
1 **tablespoon prepared mustard**
Salt and pepper to taste
12 **large pimiento-stuffed olives, halved widthwise**

1. Place eggs in a single layer in a large saucepan; add enough water to cover by 1 in. Cover and bring to a boil over high heat. Remove from the heat; cover and let stand for 15 minutes. Place in ice water until completely cooled. Gently crack eggs (do not peel).

2. Fill a large bowl with hot water; add the food coloring to tint water a dark red. Add eggs, making sure they are completely covered by water; let stand for 30 minutes. Remove eggs from water; peel (eggs should have a veined appearance).

3. Cut eggs in half widthwise; place yolks in a large bowl. Set whites aside. Mash yolks with a fork; stir in the mayonnaise, mustard, salt and pepper.

4. To make eggs stand better on the serving plate, slice a small piece from the bottom of egg white halves. Stuff with yolk mixture. Place an olive half in the center of each to resemble an eyeball. Refrigerate until serving.

Frankie Cupcakes

Boo-Ya Mini Pizzas

Here's what I call party food! These individual pizzas are super cute and use simple ingredients.

—POLLY COUMOS MOGADORE, OH

START TO FINISH: 25 MIN.
MAKES: 20 MINI PIZZAS

- 2 **tubes (12 ounces each) refrigerated buttermilk biscuits**
- 1 **can (8 ounces) tomato sauce**
- 1½ **teaspoons dried minced onion**
- 1 **teaspoon dried oregano**
- 1 **teaspoon dried basil**
- ⅛ **teaspoon garlic powder**
- 20 **slices part-skim mozzarella cheese**
  Sliced ripe olives

1. Preheat oven to 400°. Roll or pat biscuits into 2½-in. circles. Place on greased baking sheets.
2. In a small bowl, combine the tomato sauce, onion, oregano, basil and garlic powder; spread over biscuits. Bake 8-10 minutes or until edges are lightly browned.
3. Meanwhile, using a small ghost-shape cookie cutter, cut a ghost out of each cheese slice. Immediately place a ghost over each pizza; add pieces of olives for faces.

HOW TO

DECORATE A SCARY PARTY

❶ Grab some old white bedsheets and draw ghostly eyes and a mouth on each of them. Drape the sheets over the bristle ends of brooms, propping the ghosts against a wall.
❷ For an eerie glow, replace some of the lightbulbs in your home with green or orange bulbs.
❸ Purchase a bag of spider webbing from a party supply store, then drape the webbing over tables, mantels and counters.

Boo-Ya Mini Pizzas

Give Thanks for Tasty Treats

CORNUCOPIA SNACKS

These treats are irresistible to guests of any age. First, whip up a sweet snack mix of your choice—I use honey-roasted peanuts, Cinnamon Burst Cheerios and dried fruit. Roll waffle cones in melted semisweet chocolate, then in gold sanding sugar. Rest the cones on waxed paper. When set, fill with snack mix and nibble away.

—MANDY HEASTON
GREELEY, CO

Head to Mandy's blog for more clever holiday eats.
gourmetmomonthego.com

Pretzel Turkey Treats

Send your holiday guests home with these delightful edible favors.

—LORRI REINHARDT BIG BEND, WI

PREP: 2 HOURS + STANDING
MAKES: 1 DOZEN

- 6 **Fruit by the Foot fruit rolls**
- 9 **circus peanut candies**
- 1 **cup butterscotch chips, divided**
- 24 **candy eyeballs**
- 6 **chocolate-covered thin mints**
- 12 **large sourdough pretzels**
- 36 **milk chocolate kisses, unwrapped**
- 12 **vanilla wafers**

1. Using kitchen scissors, cut feathers and 12 wattles from fruit rolls. Cut three circus peanuts crosswise in half. Cut 24 turkey feet from remaining circus peanuts.

2. Reserve 12 butterscotch chips for beaks. In a microwave, melt ½ cup of the remaining chips; stir until smooth. Using melted chips, attach two candy eyeballs, a wattle and a beak to each halved circus peanut. Repeat, using thin mints for remaining heads.

3. Place a pretzel on a waxed paper-lined microwave-safe plate. Place a chocolate kiss in each of the three holes. Microwave on high for 15-20 seconds or until melted. While still warm, arrange feathers in a fan shape over pretzel, pressing gently into melted chocolate to adhere. Repeat with remaining pretzels and kisses.

4. Melt remaining butterscotch chips. Using melted chips, attach a vanilla wafer to each pretzel for body; attach heads. Attach circus peanut pieces for feet. Let stand until set.

Pretzel Turkey Treats

Turkey Focaccia Club

My family thinks this sandwich is pure heaven, thanks to the cranberry-pecan mayo. I'm asked to make this all year long!

—JUDY WILSON SUN CITY WEST, AZ

START TO FINISH: 20 MIN.
MAKES: 4 SERVINGS

- ½ cup mayonnaise
- ½ cup whole-berry cranberry sauce
- 2 tablespoons chopped pecans, toasted
- 2 tablespoons Dijon mustard
- 1 tablespoon honey
- 1 loaf (8 ounces) focaccia bread
- 3 lettuce leaves
- ½ pound thinly sliced cooked turkey
- ¼ pound sliced Gouda cheese
- 8 slices tomato
- 6 bacon strips, cooked

1. In a small bowl, mix the first five ingredients until blended. Using a long serrated knife, cut focaccia horizontally in half. Spread cut sides with mayonnaise mixture. Layer bottom half with lettuce, turkey, cheese, tomato and bacon; replace bread top. Cut into wedges.

NOTE *To toast nuts, bake in a shallow pan in a 350° oven for 5-10 minutes or cook in a skillet over low heat until lightly browned, stirring occasionally.*

Turkey Cheese Ball

While the main turkey is roasting, you can present loved ones with this Thanksgiving cheese ball. It can also be set out as a stunning centerpiece for your holiday table.

—*TASTE OF HOME* TEST KITCHEN

PREP: 45 MIN. + CHILLING
MAKES: 1 CHEESE BALL (3 CUPS)

- 2 packages (8 ounces each) reduced-fat cream cheese
- 6 ounces deli smoked turkey, finely chopped
- 1 cup (4 ounces) shredded cheddar cheese
- 1 tablespoon finely chopped onion
- 1 tablespoon Worcestershire sauce
- ½ teaspoon garlic powder

DECORATIONS

- 3 packages (3 ounces each) cream cheese, softened
- 2 tablespoons 2% milk

Turkey Cheese Ball

Brown, orange and yellow paste food coloring
- 6 large oval crackers
- 1 large sweet red pepper
- 1 small yellow summer squash
- 1 cup pecan halves
  Assorted crackers

1. In a small bowl, beat the first six ingredients until combined. Shape the mixture into a ball; wrap in plastic wrap. Refrigerate for 1 hour or until firm.

2. In another small bowl, beat cream cheese and milk until smooth. Divide among four small bowls. With food coloring, tint one bowl brown, one dark orange and one light orange (using yellow and orange); leave one bowl plain.

3. Transfer each mixture to a heavy-duty resealable plastic bag; cut a small hole in a corner of each bag.

4. For turkey tail feathers, decorate the top halves of large oval crackers with tinted cream cheese.

5. Cut the red pepper to form the turkey head, neck and wattle. For beak, cut a small triangle from summer squash; attach with cream cheese. Add eyes, using brown and plain cream cheese. Insert pecan halves and decorated crackers into cheese ball. Serve with assorted crackers.

NOTE *This recipe was tested with Townhouse Oval Bistro crackers.*

DID YOU KNOW?

Chopping onions make you cry every time? If you freeze the onions for about 20 minutes, they shouldn't make your eyes water when it's time to chop.

Pumpkin Mousse Dip

½ cup finely chopped nuts
1 can (16 ounces) vanilla frosting
2 packages (16 ounces each) Reese's pieces
Dried corn husks

1. Prepare cake batter according to package directions; add nuts. Grease and flour a 9-in. round baking pan; add batter and bake as directed. Cool for 10 minutes.

2. Remove cake from pan to a wire rack to cool completely. Freeze the cake for easier cutting. Cut the cake into ears of corn using the diagram found below. Set aside the remaining cake for another use.

3. Place cakes on a serving platter or covered board. Frost tops and sides with 1½ cups frosting. Decorate tops, sides and bottom ends of each ear with Reese's pieces. Cut corn husks into 8- to 12-in. lengths. Attach to cakes using additional frosting. Gently pull the husks together in the middle and tie with twine.

NOTE *Don't have Reese's pieces candies on hand? Try decorating the cakes with M&M's or candy corn instead. To make individual treats for guests, simply form mini corncobs by cutting smaller pieces of cake and corn husks.*

FINISHED SIZE *Not including corn husks, the middle cake shown in the photo measures about 8 inches long x 3 inches wide, and each side cake measures about 6 inches long x 2½ inches wide.*

Pumpkin Mousse Dip

I got this recipe from my daughter's Girl Scout leader. The fluffy pumpkin dip is especially delicious when served with gingersnaps, pear slices, apple slices or graham crackers.
—**MARY SLATER** BELPRE, OH

START TO FINISH: 10 MIN.
MAKES: 16 SERVINGS (¼ CUP EACH)

1 cup canned pumpkin
½ cup confectioners' sugar
1 package (3 ounces) cream cheese, softened
½ teaspoon ground cinnamon
1 carton (8 ounces) frozen whipped topping, thawed
Gingersnap cookies and/or pear slices

In a large bowl, beat the pumpkin, sugar, cream cheese and cinnamon until smooth. Fold in the whipped topping. Refrigerate until serving. Serve with gingersnaps and pear slices.

Harvest Corn Cakes

Sweet corn takes on a whole new meaning with this recipe. They look delightfully like the real deal but they're made of cake, frosting and Reese's pieces. Children have fun putting the "kernels" on—and eating a few as well!
—**MARY DETWEILER** MIDDLEFIELD, OH

PREP: 40 MIN. • **BAKE:** 35 MIN. + COOLING
MAKES: 8 SERVINGS

1 package (9 ounces) yellow cake mix

HARVEST CORN CAKES DIAGRAM

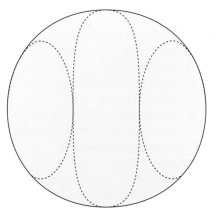

Harvest
Corn Cakes

Three Cheers for Dessert!

It's finally time for everyone's favorite part of a meal: dessert, of course! Wow the crowd at your next bake sale, birthday party or potluck with these sweets.

Xylophone Cakes

Give a Hoot Cupcakes

Hoot hoot! Party guests will be eyeing these treats long before you set them out. They make a lasting impression and require only six ingredients.

—*TASTE OF HOME* TEST KITCHEN

PREP: 45 MIN. • **MAKES:** VARIES

> Cupcakes of your choice
> 1 can (16 ounces) chocolate frosting
> Oreo cookies
> ¼ cup vanilla frosting
> Chocolate-covered peppermint candies
> Small banana-shaped hard candies (Runts)

1. Frost the cupcakes with chocolate frosting.
2. Split the sandwich cookies in half, keeping the cream side whole (microwaving a few cookies at a time for several seconds helps to keep the cream side solid when splitting). Place cookies, cream side up, on cupcakes for eyes. Cut remaining cookie pieces crosswise into thirds; discard the center third and set the rest aside.
3. With the vanilla frosting, attach the chocolate-covered mints for eyes; pipe pupils.
4. Place reserved cookie pieces above eyes for the ears. Pipe chocolate frosting on ears and around eyes.
5. For beaks, press yellow candies between the eyes.

Xylophone Cakes

Our son, Alex, came home from school one day and told me it was his turn to bring in a snack for the letter of the week, which happened to be "X." My husband came up with the idea of the xylophone cakes, to the delight of Alex, his classmates and his teacher.

—**MICHELE CASCAIS** MENDHAM, NJ

PREP: 40 MIN. • **MAKES:** 14 CAKES

> 2 loaves (10¾ ounces each) frozen pound cake, thawed
>   Yellow, green, orange and red gel food coloring
> 1 can (16 ounces) vanilla frosting
>   M&M's minis
> 28 miniature marshmallows
> 28 pretzel sticks

1. Cut each cake widthwise into seven 1-in. slices. Trim a diagonal slice from the long sides of each slice, angling slightly, leaving a 1-in. width at one short end.
2. Use food coloring to tint the frosting. Carefully spread or pipe stripes on cake slices; top with

M&M's. For mallets, press a miniature marshmallow into one end of each pretzel stick.

Candy "Onion" Rings

Fool even the most seasoned foodie with this basket of candy "onion" rings. Graham cracker crumbs coat Twizzlers to create the illusion of deep-fried goodness.

—*TASTE OF HOME* TEST KITCHEN

PREP: 20 MIN. + STANDING
MAKES: 10 SERVINGS

> 10 licorice pastels
> 10 pieces Twizzlers Rainbow Twists
> 5 ounces white candy coating, melted
> ¾ cup graham cracker crumbs

1. Place a pastel in the end of a twist. Attach the other end of twist to pastel, forming a ring. Repeat with remaining pastels and twists.
2. Place melted coating and cracker crumbs in separate shallow bowls. Dip rings in coating, allowing excess to drip off, then roll in crumbs. Place on waxed paper; let stand until set.

Give a Hoot Cupcakes

Crisp Button Cookies

Almost too cute to eat but too tasty to resist, these clever cookies take only minutes to make. They'll disappear even more quickly.

—**BONNIE BUCKLEY** KANSAS CITY, MO

PREP: 20 MIN. + CHILLING
BAKE: 10 MIN./BATCH
MAKES: ABOUT 3 DOZEN

- ¾ **cup butter, softened**
- 1 **cup confectioners' sugar**
- 1 **egg**
- 1 **teaspoon vanilla extract**
- 2½ **cups all-purpose flour**
- ¼ **teaspoon salt**
- ¼ **teaspoon ground cardamom**
  Assorted food coloring, optional
  Multicolored pull-and-peel licorice

1. In a large bowl, cream butter and confectioners' sugar until light and fluffy. Beat in egg and vanilla. In another bowl, whisk flour, salt and cardamom; gradually beat into creamed mixture. If desired, divide dough into portions; tint with food coloring. Refrigerate, covered, 2 hours or until easy to handle.

2. Preheat oven to 350°. On a lightly floured surface, roll dough to ¼-in. thickness. Cut with a floured 2½-in. round cookie cutter. Place 1 in. apart on ungreased baking sheets. With the top of a ¼-cup measuring cup dipped in flour, press an indented edge into each cookie. Using a plastic straw, cut out four holes near the center of the cookie.

3. Bake 10-15 minutes or until edges are lightly browned. Remove to wire racks to cool. Lace licorice through the holes in each button; trim licorice.

DID YOU KNOW?

Confused about the difference between confectioners' sugar and powdered sugar? They're actually the same thing! Some cooks use one name instead of the other, but *Taste of Home* recipes stick with the term "confectioners' sugar."

Crisp Button Cookies

Lady Bug Chocolate Cupcakes

Green Sherbet Froggie

This sublime snack in disguise will make you want to hop right to dessert. It's like summer in a dish.

—*TASTE OF HOME* TEST KITCHEN

START TO FINISH: 10 MIN.
MAKES: 1 SERVING

- 1 scoop lime sherbet
- 3 green grapes (2 small and 1 large), halved lengthwise
- 2 fresh blueberries
  Green decorating gel or icing

1. Just before serving, place a rounded scoop of sherbet on an individual serving dish. Position small grape halves for legs.
2. For eyes, insert large grape halves into sherbet; add blueberries for eyeballs. Draw a smile with decorating gel. Serve immediately.

Lady Bug Chocolate Cupcakes

Who wouldn't smile upon seeing these fun little cupcakes sitting on the kitchen table? They'll fly off your serving platter!

—*TASTE OF HOME* TEST KITCHEN

PREP: 30 MIN. • **BAKE:** 25 MIN. + COOLING
MAKES: 14 CUPCAKES

- ½ cup butter, softened
- 1 cup sugar
- 1 egg
- 1 teaspoon vanilla extract
- 1½ cups all-purpose flour
- ½ cup baking cocoa
- 1 teaspoon baking soda
- ¼ teaspoon salt
- ½ cup buttermilk
- ½ cup strong brewed coffee
  Chocolate wafer cookies
- 1 can (16 ounces) dark chocolate fudge frosting
  Red jimmies
  Black jelly beans, shoestring licorice and nonpareils and white hard candies

1. In a small bowl, cream butter and sugar until light and fluffy. Beat in egg and vanilla. Combine the flour, cocoa, baking soda and salt; gradually add to creamed mixture alternately with buttermilk and coffee, beating well after each addition.
2. Fill 14 paper-lined muffin cups two-thirds full. Bake at 350° for 25-30 minutes or until a toothpick inserted near the center comes out clean. Cool for 10 minutes before removing from pans to wire racks to cool completely.
3. For lady bug wings, microwave chocolate wafers for a few seconds to slightly soften. Use a serrated knife to cut each in half. Cut off the tips to allow room for the lady bug face; save remaining wafer pieces to prop up wings. Frost both wings and dip in red jimmies. Cut black jelly beans in half; add as spots to the wings. Set aside.
4. For antennae, cut licorice into 1-in. pieces. Dip one end into the frosting and roll in black nonpareils; set aside to dry.
5. To assemble cupcake, frost with chocolate icing. Position decorated wings on cupcakes; if desired, add reserved wafer piece under wing tip to prop up. Add the antennae and white hard candy eyes. Pipe a small frosting dot for eyeballs. Add a large curved red jimmie and two small ones for the mouth.

Green Sherbet Froggie

Monkey Cupcakes

Kids' eyes will light up when they see these cute jungle goodies. The cupcakes never fail to make my grandkids smile, and they're always a huge hit at bake sales.
—**SANDRA SEAMAN** GREENSBURG, PA

PREP: 30 MIN. • **BAKE:** 20 MIN. + COOLING
MAKES: 2 DOZEN

- 1 package chocolate cake mix (regular size)
- 1 can (16 ounces) chocolate frosting
- 24 vanilla wafers
  Black and red decorating gel
- 48 pastel blue and/or green milk chocolate M&M's
- 12 Nutter Butter cookies

1. Prepare batter and bake according to package directions for cupcakes; cool completely.

2. Set aside ¼ cup frosting. Frost cupcakes with remaining frosting. With a serrated knife, cut off and discard a fourth of each vanilla wafer. Place a wafer on each cupcake, with the rounded edge of wafer near edge of cupcake, for face. Add dots of black gel for nostrils. With red gel, pipe on mouths.

3. Place M&M's above wafers for eyes; add dots of black gel for pupils. Using reserved frosting and a #16 star tip, pipe hair. Carefully separate cookies; cut each in half. Position one on each side of cupcakes for ears.

Going Bananas

These tempting cutout cookies can be made to suit any holiday or occasion. As adorable bananas, they suit a monkey-themed party very well.
—**SHARON SKILDUM** MAPLE GROVE, MN

PREP: 30 MIN. • **BAKE:** 10 MIN.
MAKES: ABOUT 3 DOZEN

- 1 cup butter, softened
- 1¼ cups sugar
- 3 eggs
- 1 teaspoon vanilla extract
- ½ teaspoon almond extract
- 3½ cups all-purpose flour
- 1 teaspoon baking powder
- ½ teaspoon salt

ICING
- 2 cups confectioners' sugar
- 1 tablespoon meringue powder
- ¼ cup warm water
- ½ teaspoon almond extract
  Yellow and brown paste food coloring

1. In a large bowl, cream butter and sugar until light and fluffy. Add eggs, one at a time, beating well after each addition. Beat in extracts. Combine the flour, baking powder and salt; gradually add to creamed mixture. Cover and refrigerate for 1 hour or until easy to handle.

2. On a lightly floured surface, roll out dough to ¼-in. thickness. Cut dough with a floured 4x1-in. banana- or crescent-shaped cookie cutter. Place 1 in. apart on lightly greased baking sheets. Bake at 375° for 8-10 minutes or until lightly browned. Remove to wire racks to cool.

3. For the icing, sift confectioners' sugar and meringue powder into a small bowl. Add water and extract; beat on low speed until blended. Beat on high for 4-5 minutes or until stiff peaks form.

4. Tint 3 tablespoons icing brown. Keep unused icing covered at all times with a damp cloth. Place brown icing in a pastry bag. Using a #3 round pastry tip, pipe the outline and stems of the banana.

5. Tint remaining icing with yellow food coloring. Add water, a few drops at a time, until mixture is thin enough to flow smoothly. Fill in the center space of each cookie, allowing the icing to spread to the outline. Let dry overnight. Store in airtight containers.
NOTE *Meringue powder is available from Wilton Industries. Call 800-794-5866 or visit* **wilton.com.**

Monkey Cupcakes
& Going Bananas

Autumn Leaf Cutouts

Autumn Leaf Cutouts

Classic cookies become autumn leaves in this delectable recipe. Make them in solid colors or combine pieces of tinted dough for a multicolored effect.
—**DARLENE BRENDEN** SALEM, OR

PREP: 25 MIN. + CHILLING
BAKE: 15 MIN./BATCH + COOLING
MAKES: 4 DOZEN

- 2 **cups butter, softened**
- 1½ **cups sugar**
- 2 **eggs**
- 2 **teaspoons vanilla extract**
- 5½ **cups all-purpose flour**
- ½ **teaspoon baking soda**
- ½ **teaspoon salt**
  Red, green, orange and yellow paste food coloring
- 1⅓ **cups confectioners' sugar**
- 5 **to 7 teaspoons warm water**
- 1 **tablespoon meringue powder**
- ¼ **teaspoon almond extract**
- 2 **tablespoons coarse sugar**

1. In a large bowl, cream butter and sugar until light and fluffy. Beat in eggs and vanilla. In another bowl, whisk flour, baking soda and salt; gradually beat into creamed mixture.
2. Divide dough into four portions; tint one red, one green, one orange and one yellow. Shape each into a disk; wrap in plastic wrap. Refrigerate 30 minutes or until firm enough to roll.

3. Preheat oven to 350°. On a lightly floured surface, roll each portion of dough to ¼-in. thickness. Cut with a floured 3-in. leaf-shaped cookie cutter. Place 2 in. apart on greased baking sheets.
4. Bake 14-17 minutes or until edges are golden brown. Remove from pans to wire racks to cool completely.
5. Meanwhile, in a large bowl, combine confectioners' sugar, water, meringue powder and almond extract; beat on low speed just until blended. Pipe or drizzle on cookies as desired. Sprinkle with coarse sugar. Let stand until set. Store in an airtight container.

Bird Nests

I found one more thing to love about Peeps, the perennial springtime favorite: They make perfect mother birds for these pretzel nests with candy eggs.
—**JESSICA BOIVIN** NEKOOSA, WI

PREP: 40 MIN. • **MAKES:** 25 SERVINGS

- 2 **packages (10 to 12 ounces each) white baking chips**
- 1 **package (10 ounces) pretzel sticks**
- 25 **yellow chick Peeps candy**
- 1 **package (12 ounces) M&M's eggs or other egg-shaped candy**

1. In a large microwave-safe bowl, melt white chips; stir until smooth. Set aside ½ cup for decorating.

2. Add pretzel sticks to remaining chips; stir until coated. Scoop a small amount of mixture onto waxed paper; shape into a nest using two forks. Repeat, forming 25 nests. Dip bottom of a Peep into reserved white chips; place in a nest. Add eggs to nests, securing with white chips. Repeat. Let stand until set.

Petal Cupcakes

You just need a few pantry ingredients to whip up pretty flowers to top cupcakes.
—**TASTE OF HOME** TEST KITCHEN

PREP: 20 MIN. • **MAKES:** VARIES

- 1 **can (16 ounces) vanilla frosting**
  Lavender food coloring
  Cupcakes of your choice
  Large and miniature marshmallows
  Lavender colored sugar
  Good & Plenty candies, optional

1. Tint frosting lavender; frost the cupcakes.
2. With kitchen scissors, cut marshmallows in half at an angle. Dip each cut side in colored sugar. Arrange large marshmallow petals on cupcakes, forming flowers. Add miniature marshmallow petal centers.
3. If desired, add candy stamens to center of flowers.

Petal Cupcakes

Crispy Cone Treats

Kids get a kick out of ice cream cones filled with a sweet, peanutty rice cereal mixture. They can sub for birthday cake at a party.

—VERA MATHESON PORTAGE LA PRAIRIE, MB

PREP: 20 MIN. + STANDING
MAKES: 1½ DOZEN

- 1 cup packed brown sugar
- 1 cup light corn syrup
- 1 cup peanut butter
- 1 tablespoon butter
- 4 cups crisp rice cereal
- 1 cup chopped peanuts
- 18 ice cream cake cones and/or sugar cones
- 1½ cups semisweet chocolate chips
- 1 tablespoon shortening
  Assorted jimmies

1. In a large microwave-safe bowl, combine the brown sugar, corn syrup, peanut butter and butter. Microwave on high for 1-2 minutes or until melted, stirring twice. Stir in the cereal and peanuts. Spoon into ice cream cones.

2. Melt the chocolate chips and shortening; stir until smooth. Dip tops of cones in melted chocolate, then in jimmies. Let stand until set. These treats are best served the day they are made.

Crispy Cone Treats

Favorite Ice Cream Tacos

Tacos for dessert? Why not! These ice cream-filled treats are fun to make and eat. Kids and adults alike have a ball putting them together.

—NANCY ZIMMERMAN

CAPE MAY COURT HOUSE, NJ

PREP: 30 MIN.
BAKE: 10 MIN./BATCH + COOLING
MAKES: 16 TACOS

- ½ cup packed brown sugar
- ⅓ cup butter, melted
- ¼ cup honey
- ¾ cup all-purpose flour
- ½ teaspoon water
- 4 to 5 drops green food coloring
- 1 cup flaked coconut
- ½ gallon chocolate ice cream
- 1 cup whipped topping
  Red, orange, and yellow M&M's minis

1. Using a pencil, draw two 3-in. circles on a sheet of parchment paper. Place paper, pencil mark side down, on a baking sheet; set aside.

2. In a large bowl, beat the brown sugar, butter and honey until blended. Add flour; mix well (batter will be thick). Spread 1 tablespoon of batter over each circle.

3. Bake at 350° for 6-7 minutes or until golden brown. Cool for 2 minutes. Loosen each cookie and curl around a rolling pin to form a taco shell. Cool completely before removing to a wire rack. Repeat with remaining batter.

4. In a small resealable plastic bag, combine water and food coloring; add coconut. Seal bag and shake to tint. Fill taco shells with ice cream; garnish with whipped topping, coconut and M&M's.

TAKE A DIP

Roll the classic ice cream sandwich into any sweet treat you like, such as jimmies, sprinkles, Teddy Grahams, toasted coconut, Swedish fish or crushed candy bars or Oreos. This slam-dunk of an ice cream treat will have the whole gang screaming for seconds.

Sunshine Cupcakes

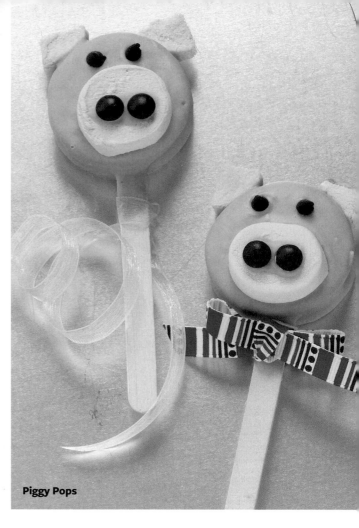

Piggy Pops

Sunshine Cupcakes

Cheery lemon cupcakes always bring lots of grins. Stock up on candy corn when it's on sale after Halloween so you can make these all year long.
—*TASTE OF HOME* **TEST KITCHEN**

PREP: 20 MIN. • **BAKE:** 20 MIN. + COOLING
MAKES: 2 DOZEN

- 1 **package lemon cake mix (regular size)**
- 1 **can (16 ounces) vanilla frosting**
  Yellow food coloring
  Miniature semisweet chocolate chips, red shoestring licorice and candy corn

1. Prepare cake batter mix according to package directions for cupcakes; cool completely.
2. In a small bowl, tint frosting yellow. Frost cupcakes. Press two chocolate chips into each cupcake for eyes. For mouths, cut licorice into 1-in. pieces; bend slightly to curve. Press one licorice piece into each cupcake. Add candy corn around edges of cupcakes.

Piggy Pops

My mother-in-law and I made these cute cookie pops for a bake sale. Wrap them in little cellophane bags and tie off with a piece of pink crafting pipe cleaner. You can curl the pipe cleaner around a pencil to make a squiggly pig's tail. Anyone with a sweet tooth will go hog wild for a chance to try one!
—**LORRI REINHARDT** BIG BEND, WI

PREP: 1 HOUR + COOLING
MAKES: 32 POPS

- 16 **large pink and/or white marshmallows**
- 1 **tablespoon sugar**
- 2 **packages (10 to 12 ounces each) white baking chips**
- 2 **tablespoons shortening**
- 3 **to 4 drops red food coloring, optional**
- 32 **double-stuffed Oreo cookies**
- 32 **wooden pop sticks or craft sticks**
- 64 **miniature semisweet chocolate chips (about 1 tablespoon)**
- 64 **M&M's miniature baking bits (about 2 tablespoons)**

1. Cut marshmallows into thirds horizontally; cut the center portion of each into four wedges for ears. Roll cut sides of ears in sugar to prevent sticking together. Set ears and remaining portions aside.
2. In a microwave, melt baking chips and shortening; stir until smooth. Stir in food coloring if desired.
3. Twist apart the sandwich cookies. Dip the end of a wooden pop stick into melted baking chip mixture and place on a cookie half; replace cookie top. Repeat. Place pops on waxed paper-lined baking sheets; refrigerate for 10 minutes or until set.
4. Reheat baking chip mixture if necessary; dip a pop in mixture and allow excess to drip off. Return to waxed paper-lined baking sheet. While wet, position a marshmallow slice on the cookie for a snout. Add ears on top edge of cookie; hold for a few seconds or until set. Add chocolate chip eyes. Place two baking bits on snout, securing with a dab of baking chip mixture. Repeat. Let stand until set.

Sugar Cookie Tarts

These little tarts are fancy enough for an elegant occasion yet they are so simple to make. Fresh fruit tastes the best, but you can substitute canned if you're in a pinch.

—**BARB WHITE** LIGONIER, PA

PREP: 20 MIN. + CHILLING
MAKES: 4 SERVINGS

- 1 **teaspoon cornstarch**
- 3 **tablespoons water**
- 2 **tablespoons orange juice**
- 1 **tablespoon lemon juice**
  Dash salt
- 5 **tablespoons sugar, divided**
- 3 **ounces cream cheese, softened**
- 4 **large sugar cookies (3 inches)**
  Assorted fresh fruit

1. For glaze, in a small saucepan, whisk the first five ingredients until smooth; stir in 3 tablespoons sugar. Bring to a boil over medium heat; cook and stir 2 minutes or until thickened. Cool slightly.

2. In a small bowl, mix cream cheese and remaining sugar until smooth. Spread over cookies. Arrange fruit over top; brush or drizzle with glaze. Refrigerate 1-2 hours or until cold.

Flutter By Cupcakes

It doesn't take magic ingredients or complicated instructions to add butterflies to the top of cupcakes. You probably have most of these items on hand right now, and the directions are easy enough for the kids to run the show.

—*TASTE OF HOME* TEST KITCHEN

PREP: 15 MIN. • **MAKES:** VARIES

- 1 **can (16 ounces) vanilla frosting**
  Green food coloring
  Cupcakes of your choice
  Miniature pretzels
  Froot Loops
  Milk chocolate M&M's
  Shoestring black licorice, cut into ⅜-inch pieces

1. Tint the frosting light green; generously frost cupcakes.

2. Position two miniature pretzels for butterfly wings. For the body, arrange four Froot Loops vertically in a row between the wings. Add an M&M head and licorice antennae.

Sugar Cookie Tarts

Fire Truck Cookies

Place ¼ cup frosting in each of two small bowls. Tint one red and the other yellow. Spread yellow frosting on the bottoms of 20 vanilla wafers; top with a peppermint patty. Spread with red frosting. Brush tops of the remaining vanilla wafers with corn syrup; sprinkle with sesame seeds. Place over red frosting.

Best Friend Cupcakes

These little pups are double the fun when served with Scooby-Doo! graham cracker sticks, which look like real dog treats. Kids will be begging for more.

—*TASTE OF HOME* TEST KITCHEN

PREP: 20 MIN. • **MAKES:** 2 DOZEN

- 1 **can (16 ounces) vanilla frosting**
  Tan or yellow food coloring
  Cupcakes of your choice
  Milano cookies
  Milk chocolate candy coating disks
  Yellow and brown M&M's
- 1 **tube (4¼ ounces) black decorating icing**

1. Tint frosting light tan. Generously frost cupcakes, mounding slightly off-center for the nose. Add cookies for ears.
2. Add one candy coating disk and one yellow M&M for eyes; use a brown M&M for the nose. Pipe dots of icing as pupils. Pipe a mouth.

Fire Truck Cookies

I worked together with other teachers to create this snack for a fire safety program at school.

—**RHONDA WALSH** CLEVELAND, TN

START TO FINISH: 20 MIN.
MAKES: 16 COOKIES

- 16 **whole graham crackers**
- 1 **cup vanilla frosting**
  Red paste or liquid food coloring
- 32 **Oreo cookies**
  Black shoestring licorice
- 16 **red gumdrops**

1. With a serrated knife, cut the top left- or right-hand corner off of each graham cracker at a 45° angle. Tint frosting red; frost crackers. Place two sandwich cookies on each for wheels.
2. For each truck, cut licorice into two 2½-in. pieces, five ½-in. pieces and two 1½-in. pieces. Place the large pieces parallel to each other above wheels, with the small pieces between to form a ladder. Place the medium pieces at cut edge, forming a windshield. Add a gumdrop for a light.

Hamburger Cookies

My husband loves peppermint patties, and our son is crazy for vanilla wafers. So I put the two together to make a cool cookie that looks just like a burger. Both my guys give the recipe a thumbs-up!

—**JULIE WELLINGTON** YOUNGSTOWN, OH

START TO FINISH: 30 MIN.
MAKES: 20 COOKIES

- ½ **cup vanilla frosting**
  Red and yellow paste or gel food coloring
- 40 **vanilla wafers**
- 20 **peppermint patties**
- 1 **teaspoon corn syrup**
- 1 **teaspoon sesame seeds**

Best Friend Cupcakes

Pizza for Dessert

Ocean Cake

Whether it's for a pool or underwater birthday party, this fish-themed cake will reel in excited reactions.
—*TASTE OF HOME* TEST KITCHEN

PREP: 30 MIN. • **BAKE:** 25 MIN. + COOLING
MAKES: 12 SERVINGS

- 1 **package white cake mix (regular size)**
- 2⅔ **cups canned vanilla frosting**
  Blue and green Fruit Roll-Ups
  Fish candies
  Black shoestring licorice
  Candy stick

1. Prepare and bake cake according to package directions, using two greased 9-in. round baking pans. Cool for 10 minutes before removing from pans to wire racks to cool completely.
2. Spread 1⅔ cups frosting between layers and over top and sides of cake. Using the back of a spoon, make waves on the top of cake with remaining frosting.
3. Cut wave shapes out of Fruit Roll-Ups; gently press along bottom of cake. Arrange additional wave shapes and fish candies on top of cake as desired. Tie licorice on one end of candy stick to create a fishing pole.
HOW-TO *To create ocean waves in frosting, first smooth the frosting. Use the back of a spoon to make a small twisting motion in one direction. Next, move spoon over slightly and make another twist the opposite way. Repeat.*
NOTE *Cut the Fruit Roll-Ups in half vertically. Then fold in half, keeping the plastic sides together. Cut into wave shapes.*

Ocean Cake

Pizza for Dessert

At first glance, some people might think this colorful "pizza" is a savory snack, but just wait for them to taste it! Let your imagination run wild with candy toppings that look like real pizza toppings.
—**SANDY GIBBONS** OCEAN PARK, WA

PREP: 30 MIN. • **BAKE:** 15 MIN. + COOLING
MAKES: 8-10 SLICES

- 1 **tube (16½ ounces) refrigerated chocolate chip cookie dough, softened**
- 1½ **cups flaked coconut**
- 1½ **teaspoons water**
- 8 **drops yellow food coloring**
- 1 **drop red food coloring**
  Large green, red and white gumdrops
- 1 **cup (6 ounces) semisweet chocolate chips**
- 1 **cup peanut butter**
  Small black jelly beans

1. Preheat oven to 350°. Press cookie dough onto a greased 12-in. pizza pan. Bake 15-20 minutes or until deep golden brown. Cool on a wire rack.
2. Place coconut in a resealable plastic bag; add water and yellow and red food coloring. Seal bag and shake well to tint; set aside. Cut green gumdrops in half. Flatten red and white gumdrops. Using a ½-in. round cookie cutter, cut out the center of each white gumdrop.
3. In a microwave-safe bowl, melt chocolate chips; stir until smooth. Place peanut butter in another microwave-safe bowl; microwave, uncovered, on high for 1 minute or until slightly softened. Spread chocolate over cookie crust; spread with peanut butter.
4. Sprinkle with the tinted coconut. Top with green, red and white gumdrops and black jelly beans; press down gently.

Igloo Cupcakes

Have a blizzard of fun making edible igloos out of cupcakes, whipped topping and marshmallows.

—**LORRI REINHARDT** BIG BEND, WI

PREP: 45 MIN. • **BAKE:** 15 MIN. + COOLING
MAKES: 1 DOZEN

- 1 package (9 ounces) yellow cake mix
- 1 carton (8 ounces) frozen whipped topping, thawed
- 6 large marshmallows
- 1 package (16 ounces) miniature marshmallows
  Coarse white sugar and/or edible glitter, optional
  Icing decorations or bear-shaped crackers, optional

1. Prepare and bake the cake mix according to package directions for cupcakes. Cool completely. Remove cupcakes from liners.
2. Place one cupcake on a serving plate, top side down. Cover completely with ¼ cup whipped topping. Cut a large marshmallow crosswise in half. Cut each half with an apple corer to make an igloo entrance; press against cupcake.
3. Starting at the bottom, cover entire cupcake with rows of miniature marshmallows, forming an igloo. Repeat with remaining cupcakes. If desired, decorate with coarse sugar and icing decorations.
NOTE *Edible glitter and icing decorations are available from Wilton Industries. Call 800-794-5866 or visit* **wilton.com.**

TOP TIP

For an extra punch of flavor, I'll sometimes stir 1 teaspoon of vanilla extract into an 8-ounce carton of whipped topping.
—**SUSAN F.** SALEM, OR

Igloo Cupcakes

Sweet & Salty Marshmallow Popcorn Treats

Circus Cake

Sweet & Salty Marshmallow Popcorn Treats

Popcorn balls get a little salty, sweet and crunchy when you add some chocolate and then go nuts.

—**NINA VILHAUER** MINA, SD

PREP: 20 MIN. + COOLING
MAKES: ABOUT 5 DOZEN

- 4 quarts popped popcorn
- 3 cups salted peanuts
- 1 package (12.6 ounces) milk chocolate M&M's
- 1 package (16 ounces) large marshmallows
- 1 cup butter, cubed

1. In a large bowl, combine the popcorn, peanuts and M&M's. In a large saucepan, combine marshmallows and butter. Cook and stir over medium-low heat until melted. Add to popcorn mixture; mix well.

2. When cool enough to handle, shape into 2-in. popcorn balls. Let stand until firm before wrapping in plastic.

Circus Cake

This whimsical cake steals the show with its cotton candy topping, cookie-laced sides and candy decorations. Little ones will squeal with delight when they see it.

—*TASTE OF HOME* TEST KITCHEN

PREP: 30 MIN. • **BAKE:** 25 MIN. + COOLING
MAKES: 12 SERVINGS

- 1 package white cake mix (regular size)
- 1 can (16 ounces) vanilla frosting
  Nerds candies
  Miniature cream-filled chocolate sandwich cookies
  Frosted animal crackers
  Miniature marshmallows
  Cotton candy
  Lollipops

1. Prepare and bake cake according to package directions, using two greased 9-in. round baking pans. Cool for 10 minutes before removing from pans to wire racks to cool completely.

2. Spread frosting between layers and over top and sides of cake. Lightly press the Nerds, sandwich cookies and animal crackers onto sides of cake. Arrange marshmallows along edge of cake. Just before serving, arrange cotton candy and lollipops on top of cake.

Cool Watermelon Pops

The kids are going to flip with excitement when they see these picture-perfect pops.
—*TASTE OF HOME* TEST KITCHEN

PREP: 20 MIN. + FREEZING
MAKES: 28 POPS

- 2 **cups boiling water**
- 1 **cup sugar**
- 1 **package (3 ounces) watermelon gelatin**
- 1 **envelope unsweetened watermelon cherry Kool-Aid mix**
- 2 **cups refrigerated watermelon juice blend**
- 28 **freezer pop molds or 28 paper cups (3 ounces each) and wooden pop sticks**
- ⅓ **cup miniature semisweet chocolate chips**
- 2 **cups prepared limeade**
- 2 **to 3 teaspoons green food coloring, optional**

1. In a large bowl, combine water, sugar, gelatin and Kool-Aid mix; stir until sugar is dissolved. Add the watermelon juice. Fill each mold or cup with 3 tablespoons watermelon mixture. Freeze until almost slushy, about 1 hour. Sprinkle with chocolate chips. Top molds with holders. If using cups, top with foil and insert sticks through foil. Freeze.

2. In a small bowl, combine limeade and food coloring if desired. If using freezer molds, remove holders. If using paper cups, remove foil. Pour limeade mixture over tops. Return holders or foil. Freeze until firm.

Call Me Leo Cupcakes

Call Me Leo Cupcakes

Guests always roar with joy when you present these kings of the jungle. And they're a snap to make, which will make your life easier!
—*TASTE OF HOME* TEST KITCHEN

PREP: 45 MIN. • **MAKES:** 2 DOZEN

- 1 **can (16 ounces) vanilla frosting**
  Orange food coloring
- 24 **yellow cupcakes baked in orange foil liners**
  Orange Fruit Gems
  Black decorating icing
  Blue and brown M&M's miniature baking bits
  Orange, red and yellow Dots candy, cut into quarters
  Cheerios

1. Tint frosting orange; frost the cupcakes. Place a fruit gem on cupcake for face.

2. Using the black decorator icing, add miniature M&Ms for eyes and nose. Pipe a few dots for the whiskers and pipe mouth.

3. For the mane, arrange Dot quarters, rounded side facing up, around the outer edge. Add Cheerios for ears.

NOTE *Sunkist Fruit Gems were used for the faces of these lions.*

Cool Watermelon Pops

DID YOU KNOW?

Filling cupcake liners doesn't have to be a messy process. If your cupcake batter is thin, use a measuring cup to dump the batter in a liner; switch to a spring-loaded ice cream scoop if the batter is thick.

Volcano Cake

For our luau, my mom baked cake layers in three sizes of pans to form a volcanic cone. Sparkling candles and hot lava made of frosting were the cake's crowning glory.

—**CAROL WAKLEY** NORTH EAST, PA

PREP: 20 MIN. • **BAKE:** 35 MIN. + COOLING
MAKES: 12-14 SERVINGS

- **1 package yellow cake mix (regular size)**
- **2 cans (8 ounces each) crushed pineapple, drained**
- **1 cup chopped walnuts**

FROSTING
- **1 package (8 ounces) cream cheese, softened**
- **½ cup butter, softened**
- **4 cups confectioners' sugar**
- **3 to 4 tablespoons milk**
- **2 teaspoons vanilla extract**
- **½ cup baking cocoa**
  Orange and red food coloring

1. Prepare cake batter according to package directions. Stir in the pineapple and walnuts. Pour 2 cups into a greased and floured 9-in. round baking pan and 2 cups into a greased and floured 8-in. round baking pan. Pour remaining batter into a greased and floured 1½-qt. ovenproof bowl.

2. Bake the layer cakes at 350° for 18-22 minutes or until a toothpick inserted near the center comes out clean. Bake the bowl cake for 35-40 minutes or until a toothpick comes out clean. Cool for 10 minutes before removing from pans to wire racks to cool completely.

3. In a large bowl, beat cream cheese and butter until fluffy. Gradually add confectioners' sugar alternately with enough milk to achieve desired consistency. Beat in vanilla. Set aside ¾ cup frosting. Add cocoa to the remaining frosting; beat until smooth.

4. Place the 9-in. layer on a serving plate; frost with chocolate frosting. Top with 8-in. layer and bowl cake, frosting between layers. Spread the remaining chocolate frosting over top and sides of cake.

5. Divide reserved white frosting in half; tint half orange and half red. Drop by spoonfuls over the top and down the sides of cake.

Peeps Sunflower Cake

The inspiration for this cake comes from a sunflower. The yellow Peeps transform into flower petals, and the chocolate chips are arranged to resemble sunflower seeds.

—**BETHANY ELEDGE** CLEVELAND, TN

PREP: 15 MIN. • **BAKE:** 30 MIN. + COOLING
MAKES: 12 SERVINGS

- **1 package yellow cake mix (regular size)**
- **2 cans (16 ounces each) chocolate frosting**
- **19 to 20 yellow chick Peeps candies**
- **1½ cups semisweet chocolate chips**

1. Prepare and bake cake mix according to package directions, using two parchment paper-lined and greased 9-in. round baking pans. Cool in pans 10 minutes before removing to wire racks; remove paper. Cool completely.

2. If cake layers have rounded tops, trim with a long serrated knife to make level. Spread frosting between layers and over top and sides of cake.

3. For petals, arrange Peeps around edge of cake, curving slightly and being careful not to separate the chicks. For sunflower seeds, arrange chocolate chips in center of cake.

Peeps Sunflower Cake

Birthday Clown Cake

Birthday Clown Cake

I baked this cake for each of our two sons' birthdays until they became teens. Kids and adults alike clamor for it!
—**MARLENE DICK** OAKVILLE, ON

PREP: 1½ HOURS
BAKE: 25 MIN. + COOLING
MAKES: 16 SERVINGS

- 3 cups all-purpose flour
- 1½ cups sugar
- ⅔ cup baking cocoa
- 2¼ teaspoons baking powder
- 1½ teaspoons baking soda
- 1½ cups mayonnaise
- 1½ cups water
- 1½ teaspoons vanilla extract

FROSTING
- 1 cup shortening
- 1 cup butter, softened
- 8 cups confectioners' sugar
- 5 to 6 tablespoons 2% milk
- 2 teaspoons vanilla extract
  Yellow, orange, green, teal, magenta and black paste food coloring
- 10 Starburst candies
- 5 ice cream sugar cones
  Assorted candies for decorating

1. Line two greased and floured 9-in. round baking pans with waxed paper and grease the paper; set aside. In a large bowl, combine the first five ingredients. In another bowl, whisk the mayonnaise, water and vanilla until smooth; stir into dry ingredients until well blended. Transfer to the prepared pans.
2. Bake at 350° for 25-30 minutes or until a toothpick inserted near the center comes out clean. Cool for 5 minutes before removing from pans to wire racks to cool completely.
3. In a large bowl, beat shortening and butter until light and fluffy. Beat in the confectioners' sugar, milk and vanilla until smooth. Place one cake layer on a serving plate. Spread frosting between layers and over top and sides of cake.
4. Divide the remaining frosting among six small bowls. Tint each with yellow, orange, green, teal, magenta and black food coloring. Cut a hole in the corner of a pastry or plastic bag; insert round tip #3. Fill bag with

yellow frosting. Pipe ribbons and bows around tops of Starburst candies to make gifts; set aside. With black frosting, pipe "Happy Birthday" on top center of cake.
5. Place cones around top edge of cake for clown hats. On sides of cake, pipe clown faces and collars. Using a variety of frosting colors, piping tips and candies, create clown hair, faces and collars. Decorate clown hats. Place gifts around bottom edge of cake.
NOTE *Use of a coupler ring will allow you to easily change pastry tips for different designs.*

Cherry Mice

Say cheese! These sweet little mice are so cute, you'll want to take a picture.
—*TASTE OF HOME* TEST KITCHEN

PREP: 45 MIN. + CHILLING
MAKES: 2 DOZEN

- 2 cups (12 ounces) semisweet chocolate chips
- 2 teaspoons shortening

Cherry Mice

- 24 maraschino cherries with stems, well drained
- 24 milk chocolate kisses, unwrapped
- 48 almond slices

1. In a microwave, melt chocolate chips and shortening; stir until smooth. Holding each cherry by the stem, dip into chocolate mixture. Place on a sheet of waxed paper; let stand until set.
2. Reheat remaining chocolate; dip cherries again, then press onto the bottom of a chocolate kiss. For ears, place almond slices between cherry and kiss. Refrigerate until set.

TOP TIP

When a recipe calls for shortening, you should use solid shortening. Substituting oil or butter for shortening will affect the finished result of a recipe.

Marshmallow Pops

2. In a large bowl, beat the cream cheese, peanut butter and 1 cup confectioners' sugar until smooth. Fold in half of the whipped topping. Spread over crust. Sprinkle with peanut butter cups.

3. In another large bowl, beat the milk, pudding mix and remaining confectioners' sugar on low speed for 2 minutes. Let stand for 2 minutes or until soft-set. Fold in remaining whipped topping.

4. Spread over peanut butter cups. Crush remaining cookies; sprinkle over the top. Cover and chill for at least 3 hours.

Wedding Shower Cupcakes

The elegant effect of these cupcakes is created by using the same color sugar and frosting.

—*TASTE OF HOME* TEST KITCHEN

PREP: 20 MIN. • **MAKES:** VARIES

- 1 can (16 ounces) vanilla frosting
  Aqua blue food coloring or color of your choice
  Cupcakes of your choice
  Aqua blue colored sugar or color of your choice

1. Tint the frosting aqua blue or the color of your choice; set aside ¼ cup. Frost cupcakes.

2. Place colored sugar in a bowl. Holding cupcake from the bottom, gently dip each cupcake into sugar, rotating slightly to cover. With remaining frosting, pipe a variety of designs on top of cupcakes.

Wedding Shower Cupcakes

Marshmallow Pops

Hosting a children's party? Making these pops is a good activity because any age can participate in the decorating.

—**MARCIA PORCH** WINTER PARK, FL

PREP: 30 MIN. + CHILLING
MAKES: 20 SERVINGS

- 2 cups (12 ounces) semisweet chocolate chips
- 4½ teaspoons canola oil
- 40 large marshmallows
- 20 wooden pop sticks
  Toppings: assorted sprinkles, flaked coconut and ground walnuts

1. In a microwave, melt chocolate chips and oil. Stir until smooth.

2. Thread two marshmallows onto each wooden stick. Roll marshmallows in melted chocolate, turning to coat. Allow excess to drip off. Roll in the toppings of your choice. Place on waxed paper-lined baking sheets. Chill until firm.

Peanut Butter Chocolate Dessert

For me, the ideal dessert combines chocolate and peanut butter. Yum!

—**DEBBIE PRICE** LARUE, OH

PREP: 20 MIN. + CHILLING
MAKES: 12-16 SERVINGS

- 20 chocolate cream-filled chocolate sandwich cookies, divided
- 2 tablespoons butter, softened
- 1 package (8 ounces) cream cheese, softened
- ½ cup peanut butter
- 1½ cups confectioners' sugar, divided
- 1 carton (16 ounces) frozen whipped topping, thawed, divided
- 15 miniature peanut butter cups, chopped
- 1 cup cold milk
- 1 package (3.9 ounces) instant chocolate fudge pudding mix

1. Crush 16 cookies; toss with the butter. Press into an ungreased 9-in.-square dish; set aside.

**Ultimate
Candy Bar Cookies**

Ultimate
Candy Bar Cookies

I created these after Halloween, when I had way too much candy left over. You can make them with any mini chocolate candy, but if you use peanut butter cups, throw them in the freezer just before unwrapping so the chocolate won't stick to the paper.
—**TARA JOHN** PLYMOUTH, MN

PREP: 30 MIN. • **BAKE:** 10 MIN./BATCH
MAKES: 4½ DOZEN

- 7 **Butterfinger candy bars (2.1 ounces each), coarsely chopped**
- 1 **cup butter, softened**
- 2 **eggs**
- 3 **cups all-purpose flour**
- 1 **teaspoon baking powder**
- ½ **teaspoon salt**
- 27 **Reese's mini peanut butter cups**
- 27 **miniature Snickers candy bars**

1. Preheat the oven to 375°. Place Butterfinger candy bars in a food processor; process until ground. In a large bowl, cream butter and 2 cups ground candy bars until blended. Beat in eggs. In another bowl, whisk flour, baking powder and salt; gradually beat into creamed mixture.
2. Shape into 1-in. balls; roll in remaining ground candy bars. Place 2 in. apart on parchment paper-lined baking sheets. Bake 8-10 minutes or until tops are cracked.
3. Immediately press a piece of candy into the center of each cookie. Cool on pans 2 minutes. Remove to wire racks to cool.
FREEZE OPTION *Freeze cookies, layered between waxed paper, in freezer containers. To use, thaw before serving.*

Alligator Cookie Pops

These adorable cookie pops will appeal to everyone regardless of his or her feelings about reptiles. Although the pops look exotic, they use everyday ingredients.
—*TASTE OF HOME* TEST KITCHEN

PREP: 1 HOUR + STANDING
MAKES: 1 DOZEN

- 12 **circus peanut candies**
- 14 **lollipop sticks**
- 1 **package (14 ounces) green Wilton candy melts**
- 12 **Nutter Butter cookies**
- 24 **miniature semisweet chocolate chips (about ½ teaspoon)**
- 24 **semisweet chocolate chips (about 1 tablespoon)**
- ⅓ **cup white baking chips, melted**
- ⅓ **cup semisweet chocolate chips, melted**

1. Cut a slit in each circus peanut, forming a mouth. Using two lollipop sticks, prop mouths open. Let stand for 30 minutes.
2. In a microwave, melt candy melts; stir until smooth. Twist apart cookies. Dip end of a lollipop stick into melted coating and place on a cookie half; replace cookie top. Repeat. Place pops on a waxed paper-lined baking sheet; refrigerate for 10 minutes or until set.
3. Meanwhile, dip a circus peanut in coating and allow excess to drip off. Place on waxed paper. Repeat with remaining circus peanuts; let stand until set.
4. Reheat candy melts if necessary; dip a cookie pop in coating and allow excess to drip off. Insert stick into a styrofoam block to stand. While coating is wet, position a coated circus peanut on the cookie for a head. Repeat.
5. For eyes, attach a miniature chocolate chip to each chocolate chip using melted white chips. Attach to head using melted chocolate. Using remaining melted chocolate, pipe nostrils onto faces; pipe teeth with melted white chips. Let stand until set.

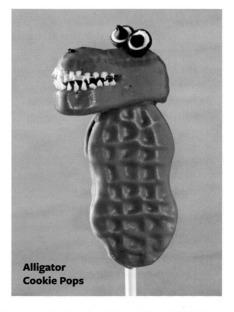

**Alligator
Cookie Pops**

**Bumblebee
Banana Cupcakes**

Jelly Bean Bark

Bumblebee
Banana Cupcakes

Everyone will make a beeline for these cute-as-a-bug cupcakes. They're wonderful for school treats, kids' parties or outdoor summer events. Start the buzz!

—**BEATRICE RICHARD** POSEN, MI

PREP: 35 MIN. • **BAKE:** 15 MIN.
MAKES: 1 DOZEN

- 1 **package (14 ounces) banana quick bread and muffin mix**
- 1 **cup milk**
- ½ **cup canola oil**
- 2 **eggs**
- 1 **can (16 ounces) vanilla frosting**
- 5 **drops yellow food coloring**
- 12 **large yellow gumdrops**
- ½ **cup chocolate frosting**
- 12 **semisweet chocolate chips**
- 24 **miniature semisweet chocolate chips, optional**
- 12 **large white gumdrops**
  Black shoestring licorice, cut into 1-inch pieces

1. In a large bowl, combine the muffin mix, milk, oil and eggs. Fill 12 greased or paper-lined muffin cups two-thirds full.

2. Bake at 375° for 15-18 minutes or until a toothpick inserted near the center comes out clean. Cool for 5 minutes before removing from pan to a wire rack to cool completely.

3. In a small bowl, combine vanilla frosting and food coloring. Frost cupcakes. Cut yellow gumdrops in half widthwise. Use the rounded tops for heads. Flatten remaining portions into ovals for bodies. Place one head and one body on each cupcake.

4. Place chocolate frosting in a resealable plastic bag; cut a small hole in a corner of the bag. Pipe stripes on the gumdrop bodies to resemble a bumblebee. For the stinger, place one chocolate chip at the end of body with pointed end facing out. Pipe two eyes with chocolate frosting or position two mini chocolate chips in front of head for eyes. Cut white gumdrops in half lengthwise; position next to bodies for wings. Insert two licorice pieces for antennae.

Jelly Bean Bark

Homemade candy really doesn't get much easier than this. You just need three ingredients, a microwave and a pan to make it happen.

—**MAVIS DEMENT** MARCUS, IA

PREP: 15 MIN. + STANDING
MAKES: 2 POUNDS

- 1 **tablespoon butter**
- 1¼ **pounds white candy coating, coarsely chopped**
- 2 **cups small jelly beans**

1. Line a 15x10x1-in. pan with foil; grease foil with butter. In a microwave, melt candy coating; stir until smooth. Spread into prepared pan. Top with jelly beans, pressing to adhere. Let stand until set.

2. Cut or break bark into pieces. Store in an airtight container.

Make-Ahead S'mores

These can be prepared ahead of time and stored. I often will pull out a few for snacks whenever unexpected company stops by.
—**ANNE SHERMAN** ORANGEBURG, SC

START TO FINISH: 20 MIN.
MAKES: 16 S'MORES

- 8 ounces semisweet chocolate, chopped
- 1 can (14 ounces) sweetened condensed milk
- 1 teaspoon vanilla extract
- 16 whole graham crackers, halved
- 2 cups miniature marshmallows

1. In a heavy saucepan, melt chocolate over low heat. Add milk; cook and stir until smooth. Stir in the vanilla. Making one s'more at a time, spread 1 tablespoon chocolate mixture over each of two graham cracker halves.
2. Place eight or nine marshmallows on one cracker; gently press the other cracker on top. Repeat. Wrap in plastic wrap; store at room temperature.

Mocha Dessert Fondue

I love to entertain, but with a full-time job and little ones at home, I don't have a lot of time. This is one of my favorite quick recipes. There's nothing like catching up with friends as we gather around a fondue pot!
—**TONYA VOWELS** VINE GROVE, KY

START TO FINISH: 15 MIN.
MAKES: 2½ CUPS

- 8 ounces semisweet chocolate, chopped
- 1 can (14 ounces) sweetened condensed milk
- ⅓ cup strong brewed coffee
  Assorted fresh fruit

In a heavy saucepan, melt chocolate with milk over low heat, stirring constantly. Stir coffee into chocolate mixture; keep warm. Serve with fruit.

Make-Ahead S'mores

General Index

This index lists every recipe by food category and/or major ingredient, so you can easily locate the recipes that best suit your tastes.

INDEXES

Alphabetical Index

This index lists all of the recipes in this book by title, making it easy to find your family's favorite dishes.